PLAYBOOK FOR SUCCESS

Using the Lessons of Sports to Win in Everything Else

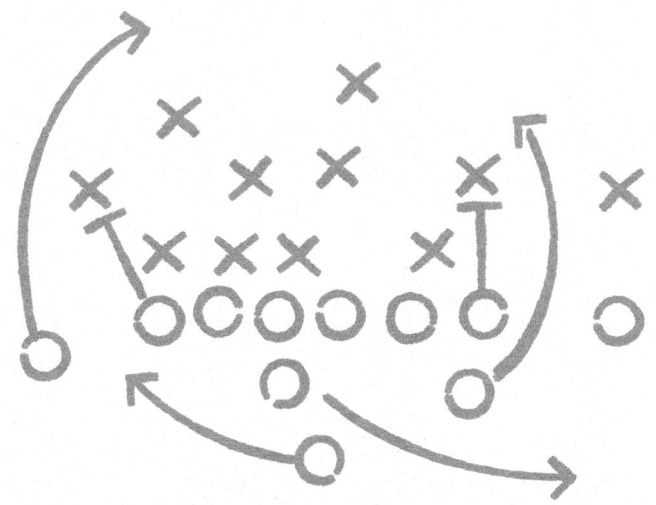

AL FLORES

ISBN (Print): 978-1-09837-870-7
ISBN (eBook): 978-1-09837-871-4

I dedicate this book to my mother and father in Heaven for the role models they were to me and for the unwavering encouragement they always provided me.

I also dedicate it to friends Lindsay Schnebly and Loren Ledin for their respected feedback and ongoing support, and Dr. Doug Lisle for his remarkable insights into the psychology of being human.

I further dedicate it to Helga for her ongoing inspiration, for being a loyal and trusted assistant, for being a great listener, for putting things in perspective, and for being a dear and wonderful friend.

And, finally, I dedicate this to the athletes and coaches who have inspired me throughout my life.

"I always turn to the sports pages first, which record people's accomplishments. The front page has nothing but man's failures."

—Earl Warren, former California governor and former chief justice of the United States Supreme Court

"Remember, results aren't the criteria for success — it's the effort made for achievement that is most important."

—John Wooden, legendary head coach of the UCLA basketball team

"People who work together will win, whether it be against complex football defenses, or the problems of modern society."

—Vince Lombardi, legendary head coach of the Green Bay Packers

CONTENTS

THE PRE-GAME SPEECH: PLAY (AND WIN) LIKE A CHAMPION

Life is hard. Every day is a series of challenges, issues, and obstacles that each of us must overcome. Things just aren't as easy as we'd like them to be.

We don't get to muddle through the day and get paid for doing nothing, though some of us—perhaps the lazy ones—spend some time trying to figure out if that is possible. But in reality, it is results that are rewarded, and it is effort that earns winning results. I'm a huge sports fan, particularly of Los Angeles-based teams, as I live in Orange County and have lived in the L.A. metropolitan area since the age of four, when my mom and dad moved our family from Johnstown, Pennsylvania.

I am now a sexagenarian and have plenty of experience watching and learning the lessons that come from sports. I am convinced my knowledge of sports has helped me to navigate everyday life.

As a college kid at the University of Southern California (USC aka SC), I became fascinated, as a journalism major, by the world going on around me. Journalism gave me the opportunity to grow from a shy teenager who didn't talk much to an inquisitive and nosy young adult who loved to observe how the world operated.

I played sports from the time I joined a Little League team at nine years of age through junior high school intramural sports, and high school basketball, baseball, and tennis teams. I actually never took a regular gym class while in junior and senior high school because I was always on a school sports team instead.

As a kid, my favorite athlete was Sandy Koufax, the Hall of Fame pitcher for the Los Angeles Dodgers. From watching Sandy, I learned the value of high character and hard work. As a left-handed pitcher myself, I used to emulate Sandy's windup—starting with my feet together on the mound and my left hand covering the ball as it sat in my glove turned up to the sky. I pictured myself being the kind of superstar that he was.

Like Sandy, I would step back with my right leg as I reached over my head with my arms together and then lift my right leg up as I angled it toward the first-base dugout, with my upper torso leaning back slightly. This would provide both leverage and inertia as my body swung forward and I moved toward home plate.

With the ball behind his head, Sandy would then whip his left arm forward in an L-shaped configuration, before snapping his forearm toward the ground to deliver the pitch; I did the same. If I could act like him, I thought, perhaps I could be successful like him. I pictured my pitches hurtling toward the plate at more than ninety miles an hour, just like his did.

It may be obvious to say that I never had Sandy's athletic prowess, but as a kid, I did learn important life lessons from watching my favorite athletes (including Jerry West of the Lakers) demonstrate the value of process, practice, and hard work. And I observed the payoff.

There's a principle in sports that you don't get what you don't work for. No one is an accidental champion. Championships are earned.

Have you ever seen the sports movie *The Legend of Bagger Vance*? Will Smith (Vance) plays a mystical, good-luck caddy who helps a local Georgian golfing hero from World War I regain his authentic swing during an exhibition match against two of the greatest golfers of the time (Walter Hagen and Bobby Jones).

With Vance's magical guidance and kind and gentle encouragement, the local golfer, Rannulph Junuh (played in the movie by Matt Damon), reaches the precipice of winning that tournament.

But Vance leaves Junuh when the pressure is heightened, at crunch time, because championships have to be earned on their own, with no help.

The best moments in sports are like that—achievable through true tests of grit, determination, hard work, and past lessons. As an injured Kirk Gibson stood in the batter's box during the ninth inning of the 1988 World Series, facing Dennis Eckersley, the best closer in baseball, he remembered the pregame advice of a Los Angeles Dodgers' scout.

"Padnah, as sure as I'm standing here breathing," Gibson recalled Mel Didier saying, "he's going to throw you a 3-2 backdoor slider."

Without the ability to push off with his legs because of the injuries that relegated him to the role of a bystander that series, Gibson focused on what became his one and only "at bat."

He remembered that pregame lesson and with only the strength of his arms, hit the game-winning home run that has been called the greatest moment in Los Angeles sports history.

Sports build character. Sports build teamwork and camaraderie. Sports build respect. And those who understand sports learn some incredible life lessons that can be employed during other important aspects of their lives.

I have believed for the majority of my life that sports are a microcosm of society in general. Every human is involved in a lifelong competitive process, and what exemplifies that better than the world of sports?

By understanding how to exist and succeed in the world of sports, you are operating from a foundation that can also lead to success in school, at your job, in your family, or in your community.

An understanding of sports—and the processes used by players, coaches, and sports administrators alike to achieve their goals—provides wonderful insight into meeting life's many challenges.

The title of this book, *Playbook for Success*, is simple enough. In football, the playbook holds all of a team's plays in it, and each player is expected to learn those plays so they can be executed flawlessly.

The ensuing chapters represent the plays of this playbook.

For me, each play illustrates a concept I learned from the sports world. For the most part, these principles are now so second nature to me that they pretty much factor into the way I live my life.

At the end of each play, or chapter, I offer a nod to the National Football League's practice of video review with a section I'm calling "After Further Review." It will recap what I hope was learned from that chapter.

We will look at concepts and philosophies passed on to us by our sports forefathers and contemporaries. With those examples, and some skillful interpretation on your part, I hope you will recognize, like me, that the precepts of sports can successfully contribute to the way you participate in the world.

Prior to every Notre Dame home football game, each player leaves the locker room by tapping a sign that reads, "Play Like a Champion Today."

It's not only a testimonial to Notre Dame's long and successful football history but also a reminder of a much-cherished goal—to play the game the right way.

Let's do *life* the same way.

PLAY #1

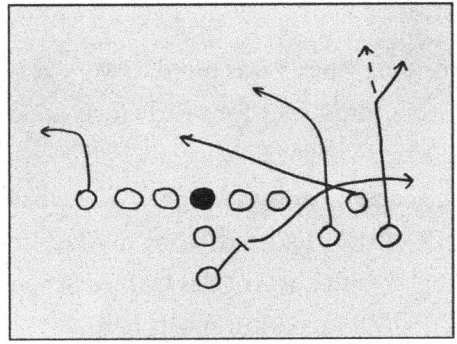

WORK HARD AND FOCUS ON
PROCESS, NOT OUTCOME

I spent my last semester at USC as the editor in chief of the *Daily Trojan* student newspaper. That experience provided my first opportunity to truly be responsible for something. And from that, I learned two critical lessons:

(1) As a leader, in order to engage your team members, you better have a vision with which they can identify.

(2) No two people are alike, and you can't expect *anyone* to think exactly like you do, or to care the same way you do.

After graduation, I worked for a small weekly newspaper in Arcadia, California, for six months, then had the opportunity to interview for a new position in the Promotions Department at the Disneyland Resort, part of the Marketing Division. This came about because of a relationship that was built while I was editor of the *Daily Trojan.*

As a kid, Disneyland was one of the only two places I dreamed of working when I grew up. The other was the Los Angeles Dodgers, mostly because of my childhood hero, Sandy Koufax, and my love for sports.

It was a blessing when I was hired to work at Disneyland, and I continued to work for Disney for nearly forty-four years until my retirement in 2019.

During my career, I always sought to demonstrate the strong, old-school work ethic I learned from my father, a blue-collar maintenance worker with Los Angeles Unified School District. And, of course, from many a successful sports hero.

Legendary Green Bay Packers football coach Vince Lombardi once said this about success:

"The only place success comes before work is in the dictionary."

Three of the most successful basketball players of all time have been Michael Jordan, who won six NBA championships, Kobe Bryant, who won five, and LeBron James, who, by the end of the 2019-2020 season, had four.

Not coincidentally, they were also known as the most hardworking players on their individual teams, setting examples for their teammates to follow. In Kobe's case, there was actually a phrase for it—Mamba Mentality—based on his nickname as the Black Mamba.

Michael Jordan once did a commercial where the catch phrase was "Be Like Mike." And LeBron James' accomplishments have earned him the moniker "The King."

After Kobe Bryant died in a helicopter crash on January 26, 2020, the Los Angeles Lakers' next game, a home game, was canceled. Instead of covering that game, the TNT network sent the crew of their

Inside the NBA show to L.A.'s Staples Center to produce a TV special they called *Remembering Kobe.*

The hosts of that show (Ernie Johnson, Charles Barkley, Kenny Smith, and Shaquille "Shaq" O'Neal) were joined by numerous other NBA athletes that played with and against Kobe.

Among those who appeared on the show were Derek Fisher and Rick Fox, who like Shaq, played alongside Kobe for three successive championships (1999-2000, 2000-2001, and 2001-2002). Fisher paired with Kobe for two more championships during the 2008-2009 and 2009-2010 seasons.

Fox described Kobe's incredible work ethic. "We were all chasing him, even his teammates. He was passionate, driven, wanting to win at all costs . . . Kobe needed that drive and pain to work hard every day—constantly, constantly, constantly."

Fox recalled how Kobe's work habits as a young player motivated his older teammates to work harder.

"We (his teammates) were working out, lifting weights before the game. He was lifting weights before *and after* the game. We thought we were beating him to the gym. He'd been there since two o'clock in the morning."

At Kobe's memorial service, Michael Jordan shared how Kobe had reached out to him early in his career to ask for advice, and how, over time, the two of them had become good friends.

"As I got to know him, I wanted to be the best big brother I could be," Jordan said. "To do that, you have to put up with the aggravation, the late-night calls or the dumb questions . . . we talked about everything. He was just trying to be a better person."

During the crazy 2019–2020 NBA season, which was halted and then restarted in a "bubble" at the Walt Disney World Resort in Florida, the Los Angeles Lakers lost their first playoff game of the opening round to the Portland Trailblazers, the NBA's hottest team during the eight seeding games that preceded the start of the playoffs.

A follow-up *Los Angeles Times* sports story detailed the sleepless night experienced by Lakers' star forward Anthony Davis, after a sub-par 8-for-24 shooting night.

In the story, Davis said he knew who would have helped him get through that night—Kobe Bryant.

Kobe was the first NBA player to mentor Davis, which began when Davis was nineteen years old and chosen to play on the 2012 U.S. Olympic team.

"I thought about: what would he say to me in this moment if I could text him and ask for advice?" Davis was quoted as saying in the *LA Times* story. "What did you see on the floor? What would he say? And the only thing I came up with that I know he would say is, 'Play harder. Leave it out on the floor. Did you play hard in Game 1? Did you leave it out on the floor?'"

What all of these anecdotes have in common is a basic theme—having the right process in place.

While only a small number of people will play sports for a living, doing things the right way should be a standard for all of us in our pursuit of individual excellence.

And the best coaches know you set expectations for *effort*, not outcome.

If we do things the right way, and put in the proper effort, we can live with whatever outcome we achieve.

On the contrary, psychologists tell us that too much emphasis on the outcome leads to the "ego trap." The ego trap occurs when you are more focused on the outcome than the process.

A good example would be the high expectations put on a child by an overbearing, unrelenting parent who tries to push his or her child to athletic super-stardom.

This creates a negative environment permeated by the fear of failure and commonly leads to an intentional lack of effort by the trapped individual, who may wither from constant pressure and criticism.

John Wooden, the ultra-successful basketball coach at UCLA, was a master at teaching process, even with the enormous pressure his program endured to sustain championship outcomes.

Wooden was known for engaging in a process so basic, he actually began with teaching his players how to tie their shoes.

He also developed a series of principles that he placed into a "pyramid" that outlined his beliefs for attaining success.

The pyramid included fifteen building blocks featuring a five-part foundation upon which everything else was held up. That foundation was anchored by the cornerstones of "industriousness" and "enthusiasm."

In describing *industriousness*, Wooden believed, "There is no substitute for work. Worthwhile results come from hard work and careful planning."

He said *enthusiasm* "brushes off upon those with whom you come in contact. You must truly enjoy what you are doing."

The other three elements of the pyramid's foundation were *friendship*, *loyalty*, and *cooperation*.

Wooden thought if you like what you are doing, and the people you are doing it with, and add some hard work and cooperative team spirit, you are laying a solid path for success.

It all sounds good to me. Besides, how do you argue with that philosophy when it comes from a man who won ten national championships in a twelve-year period?

AFTER FURTHER REVIEW: *What makes this play work?*

Nothing long-lasting is easy to accomplish. Long-running success requires extensive commitment and hard work, and the more difficult the task, the harder it is to accomplish.

An NBA championship requires a team to win four seven-game series after a long season, with each series bringing a tougher opponent.

Every human does a cost-benefit analysis when deciding what a goal is worth. Standing in a long line to vote may not appeal to some and may result in certain people passing up the opportunity, but for others, there's an incredible desire to have their voices heard. For those individuals, no matter the time involved, voting is worth the effort.

When we look at the athletes we've respected over the years (such as Michael Jordan, Kobe Bryant, and LeBron James), the one common denominator for their extraordinary success is their willingness to put in the work.

Athletes live by a routine, and establishing the right process lays the path to success. Our nonsports lives can benefit from those principles as well.

PLAY #2

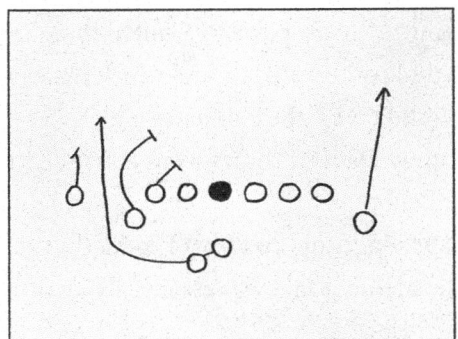

DEMONSTRATE ACCOUNTABILITY

I often talk about myself as a "sports guy." Not to tout any extraordinary personal accomplishments, but because I stay abreast of the "goings on" in the world of sports—more than most people—and live a day-to-day philosophy that is, in many ways, mirrored in sports.

To me, those philosophies make sense. I am a very practical, pragmatic thinker, and sports philosophies fall into that way of thinking, too. They translate well to our daily struggles to live and to succeed and to be loved and respected. And they are good lessons for our failures as well.

A few years ago, a popular sports phrase was not just to "talk the talk" but to also "walk the walk." In other words, follow up what you say with what you do.

In that regard, I also invest in the "work hard" philosophy and executed it during my career.

What we take on in our careers is important to us, or we wouldn't do it.

Disney has long been known for achieving excellence in its product, and I felt an accountability to the company for the role my team played in producing quality Disney product.

As a committed team player, I wanted to do my job the best I could so the payoff I contributed to, and which we achieved as a team, was the best it could be for the company.

Like Anthony Davis, I didn't want anything to fail because I didn't work hard enough.

As Senior Manager of Broadcast Production at the Disneyland Resort, I led a department that was essentially an on-site production company for the resort.

The department is unusual in the corporate world and was created in 1985 (I was involved in successfully pitching it) as a revolutionary marketing tool that is still unique today, as it is essentially a functioning television department in a nonbroadcast environment. An expensive investment. And we worked on high-profile, significant projects.

We started as a small team of five people and attempted to prove our worth and grow the team by taking on new ventures: video news releases, electronic press kits, live TV feeds on behalf of visiting TV stations, live radio remotes on behalf of visiting radio stations, B-roll video production, post-production edit bays, video archival storage, management of all on-site production at the Disneyland Resort, and the planning and execution of all broadcast activities for marketing special events, including major media events.

I retired in 2019 after the grand opening of "*Star Wars*: Galaxy's Edge," the most expensive single land ever built for a Disney theme park.

When I retired, Broadcast Production was a group of more than one hundred cast members, plus 400 broadcast-skilled consultants, and we supported projects from more than thirty different Disney clients.

Over the years, my job focused on running the team as a sort of executive producer to manage both labor and equipment resources to fulfill Disney Parks' marketing initiatives by working synergistically with numerous TV show producers, TV production companies, and news broadcast organizations who would come to the resort to shoot segments.

We coordinated all film, video, and still photography production at the resort for about 300 days of shooting a year, whether for Disney synergy programming shows (such as for ABC-TV, the Disney Channel, ESPN, Disney+, etc.) or for the marketing efforts of the Parks and Resorts division (now called Disney Parks, Experiences and Products).

Those segments would market the resort across numerous platforms and, we hoped, entice the public to visit the resort.

We specialized in planning and executing major media events, such as the one for Galaxy's Edge, where we technically produced taped and live coverage for 350 media organizations from major cities across the U.S., Canada, Mexico, Japan, the United Kingdom, Australia, and New Zealand, including broadcast and social media outlets.

There were about 40,000 individual downloads – by media organizations – of our Disney-shot, edited, and posted file footage. And more than 4,000 stories and *70 billion* media impressions were tallied during that event.

Besides the major opening executed for Galaxy's Edge, I also managed special task force broadcast teams for the grand openings of Hong Kong Disneyland Resort in 2005, Aulani Resort in Hawaii in 2011, and the Shanghai Disney Resort in 2016.

All of those required incredible individual effort to be successful. For the last three months before the opening of Galaxy's Edge, I was working twelve hours a day.

At Shanghai Disney Resort, I lived, like numerous other task force members, in a Sheraton Hotel that was forty minutes from the resort. We would be bussed to the resort and back.

For the last month, before we opened Shanghai Disney Resort, I would catch the last bus home at 8:00 p.m., get to my room by 8:50 p.m., change clothes and eat a quick dinner, then answer emails until midnight when I went to sleep (I got as many as 300 a day). Then I got back up at 5:30 a.m. to do it again.

And I wasn't the only one. My good friend Mike Hyland, who was running the public relations team's efforts—and whom my team reported to and principally supported—was doing the same thing, if not worse.

But to use a sports cliche, this was crunch time. Hard work and proper execution were imperative if we were going to be successful. As Mike liked to say, "If we work hard to lock down ninety percent of it, we can handle the ten percent that goes awry during the event itself."

Mike and I share a sports philosophy that we are only as good as our last effort. While that kind of accountability might create unwelcome pressure for some, it definitely ensured we were always attempting to do our best.

When I was leading my department, I could see the difference between a cast member who was a sports fan and one who was not.

While it is possible that a nonsports fan might have a good work ethic, it is pretty much a given that an athlete, or an invested sports fan, definitely would.

We all know those people around us who desire to coast through a workday or use the protection devices of a union membership or perhaps job seniority or some other advantage to give less than the full effort. The joke was that these people were merely "working for the weekend." To get there the easiest way possible.

Athletes know that achievement has to be earned. Those are the kind of employees you want, too. Those who earn their positions.

There is an innate understanding among those with a sports mindset about how a successful team works. Athletes (and sports fans) understand that in the team sports environment, the concept of seniority, or where you are in the pecking order, doesn't really matter.

It's all about the effort and the results.

I've always appreciated the accountability of athletes. It is not unusual to hear an athlete say after a bad game, "It's my fault. I messed up. I need to do better." But that kind of honesty is not heard enough in the nonsports setting.

When I was running my department at Disney, certain team members would have gained more respect if they had been honest in their lacking efforts and sought to redeem themselves. As humans, we have a weak spot for giving second chances and will give respect to those who accept responsibility.

Instead, I was often surprised at an individual's defensiveness or the way they put the blame on someone else, or sometimes for the response they would direct at me for bringing the incident up in the first place.

Once, we promoted a secretary to a TA (temporary assignment) role because of the great work she had done during a busy time when she came through with flying colors. I thought she had earned this assignment and was happy we could reward her.

But I was surprised when it backfired on me.

As soon as she had the better title, and increase in pay, she started becoming complacent, missing days, and not completing assignments. It was as if she thought, *I earned this. I proved my value. I can coast for a while.*

Others on the team noticed and mentioned it to me. Among the issues, she was spending a significant amount of time trying to get her son into TV commercials, and it was interfering with her work commitments.

I had a conversation with her and thought it would get better. But it didn't.

Finally, we had to make the decision to end the TA role. The cast member was incensed. She viewed it as reneging on a promise.

I remember this being the first time I used a sports analogy to explain a work situation.

I told her I had been very happy to give her a promotion because if she had been a baseball player, during the previous season she had hit over .300 and deserved the recognition.

But since then, her effort had nosedived and she was now hitting less than .200 and not contributing to the team. Worse yet, she wasn't putting in the effort and was leaving the work for others to pick up.

I said, "If this was really baseball, with that performance, we'd probably be cutting you. But it's not, and Disney is more sympathetic than that so, instead, we're simply going to end the TA and give you your old job back."

In the sports domain, athletes know they will be held accountable for their respective performances and will always be judged on what they have done lately.

But often in a corporate environment, a desire to be more compassionate usually results in those not contributing still being allowed to keep their jobs.

Another of my favorite Vince Lombardi quotes goes like this:

"Winning is not a sometime thing; it is an all the time thing. You don't do things right once in a while. You do them right all the time. Winning is habit."

That concept—employees building good habits to do their best—is a wish all business leaders have. But, unfortunately, it doesn't always happen.

An interesting example exists at Netflix to encourage positive contributions. Netflix has built its tremendous success around a culture of incredible transparency and overly honest assessments of employees. In the Netflix corporate workplace, they say, "Adequate performance gets a generous severance package."

In a 2020 *Los Angeles Times* story about his recently published book, *No Rules Rules: Netflix and the Culture of Reinvention,* Netflix co-founder Reed Hastings had this to say about how the company deals with employee performance:

"They're trusted, they're well thought of, they're well treated and the feedback can be tough. But because of that, people get better. You learn. It's kind of like exercise. You know when you do those last crunches, how it hurts? That's what makes you strong."

Accepting accountability in our personal lives, and allowing ourselves to be pushed to get better, models a sports-type philosophy. It's similar to the ice skater who spends hours in the rink, practicing a difficult jump over and over again until he or she can routinely complete it.

How good that must feel to reach that threshold!

AFTER FURTHER REVIEW: *What makes this play work?*

Psychologists will tell you that people with highly conscientious personalities will be successful. When you care, you put in the effort. And accepting accountability earns respect from your peers and more opportunities from your management. Hopefully, more money too, from those who appreciate how you have put yourself on the line.

Realize it's not enough to just "talk the talk." As the old saying goes, talk is cheap. "Walking the walk" proves your commitment to the cause and shows—when you follow through—that you can be trusted, especially during difficult circumstances.

Not accepting responsibility for your actions and blaming others or situations for your failures, or the failures of the team, ultimately gets tiring and makes it easier to justify your replacement.

Because it really is not possible for us to change our personalities, if you are struggling with a difficult situation, the best move for improving your work circumstances, as well as your personal peace of mind, may actually be a change of environment.

PLAY #3

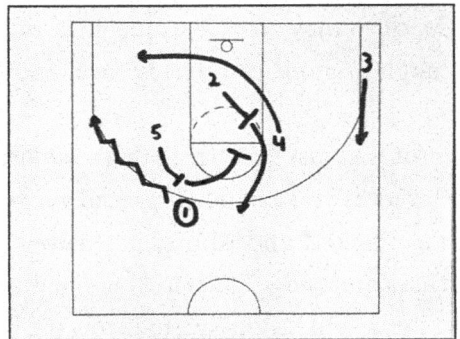

IN SPORTS, EVERYONE HAS A ROLE

While competition is inherent in sports—after all, winning is the ultimate goal—the sports culture has realized you don't have to be first string to be valuable to the team.

Though it hasn't always been that way.

In the "old days," athletes focused on the goal to be first string and sought to stand out as the "superstar" player for the pursuit of money and status. It wasn't unusual to think of a teammate as personal competition for your place in the limelight.

But over the years, coaches and astute players have come to understand that a team is only as good as its weakest link. And the team's overall success is good for everyone on it.

In a sport as violent as football, where there are plenty of injuries, coaches now talk about the "next man up" philosophy when someone gets hurt. Meaning, they need the guy who steps in for an injured teammate to give a winning effort.

If that doesn't happen, the team's chances for success will suffer.

These days, the most successful college football teams are those with the most depth so they can substitute more often and give all their players enough in-game rest to stay fresh and productive for the entire game.

That means it isn't just first string that's important. You want as many good players as you can develop. And you want to develop specialists such as "nickel" and "dime" defensive backs to thwart pass-happy offenses and "edge" pass-rushers to put pressure on a quarterback you know will be looking to throw the ball.

It just isn't efficient to have your best players play so many minutes that they can't be effective during the most crucial parts of a game.

Thus, we see the emphasis on *role players* in sports. Versatile utility players in baseball. A backup point guard in basketball. Or someone who can "hit the three" off the bench. Or a personality who provides great energy in making key "hustle" plays on the court.

One of my favorite current players for the Lakers is guard Alex Caruso.

Caruso is a fan favorite, who was a second-round pick out of Texas A&M in 2018. He's not a superstar player and is not a starter. In fact, he spent a good amount of his first two years playing on the Lakers G-League team (the NBA's minor league), but with continual improvement, he has made himself a perfect "role player" for the Lakers.

Caruso had one of the team's best "plus-minus" ratios in 2019-2020, which measures either the number of points your team outscores the other team, or the number of points your team is outscored by the other team when a specific player is on the floor.

For Caruso, this is achieved because he makes a lot of those "hustle" plays, and often the "right" play, based on the circumstances of the game.

In one of my favorite Caruso plays of 2020, one that occurred during the playoffs, he anticipated and deflected a pass intended for an opposing player near the basket, jumped in the air to catch the ball as it was sailing out of bounds, then twisted his body to toss the ball back to one of his teammates before he landed out of bounds. Whoa!

Not only did he have to anticipate what was going to happen, but he also had to get himself in position to deflect the pass, and then instantly react to put it back into play. All within a matter of seconds. And it seems like he does this every game.

Caruso is a tough defender, who uses his quick hands to disrupt an opponent's plays. He continues to build his offensive game and has a high basketball IQ, which enables him to play well alongside LeBron James, who is renowned for his own basketball IQ.

In the Game 6 win that earned the Lakers their 2020 NBA championship, Caruso contributed four points, five assists, three rebounds, one steal, and one blocked shot.

There was nothing individually spectacular about those stats, but what was noteworthy was that Caruso's overall effort allowed him to record a game-high plus-minus rating of +20. The translation: the Lakers were twenty points better than the Miami Heat when he was on the court.

Caruso is an ordinary guy who has become a star in his role.

So how does all of this translate to the nonsports world?

The best corporate department heads are those who try to get the most out of *everyone* on their teams by working to increase group morale and improve the lagging individual effort by emphasizing the importance of individual contributors to team success.

When I was building my fledgling department at Disney, free to fill the positions that were necessary for the team to be successful, I had to strategically determine what roles needed to be filled.

I needed a canny field producer, an expert cameraman, a quality audio guy, and a strong editor to bring it all together. And I needed an archivist to log and file all this footage for later retrieval. A good strong team.

Like a sports general manager, I had to evaluate where the money had to be spent on resources—both equipment and labor—and yet meet a budget. I enjoyed the process.

What wasn't fun was having to evaluate and reward individual performance in a traditional corporate environment.

And that leads us to our next chapter.

Note: "After Further Review" is deferred to include both Play #3 and Play# 4 because they are related.

PLAY #4

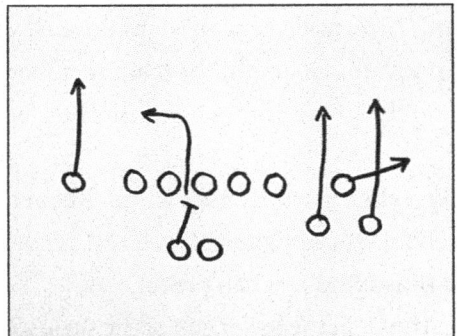

DEVELOP YOUR PLAYERS

Even the best businesses have weaknesses, and one area where companies seem to struggle is in finding effective ways to recognize and reward their employees.

Sports organizations can adequately motivate their players with contracts that offer a big salary, nice bonuses, and other desired perks and incentives which will drive achievement.

But nonsports businesses, particularly big companies, have far too many people to justify compensating the bulk of their employees that way.

This essentially creates a two-tier system, where executive level staff will earn lucrative perks, while everyone else must compete for a much-reduced level of year-end raises to determine their annual compensation. This is usually accompanied by the dreaded, mechanical, and uninspiring review.

Most companies usually don't devote a lot of time to finding a better way to reward their employees. Perhaps they think if an employee is not motivated to perform well, they don't want them anyway?

But the better companies realize that there is a substantial cost to having to find, hire, and train new employees, which makes it worthwhile to motivate and retain the team members they have.

Unfortunately, great compensation practices may still be lacking.

For many years at the Disneyland Resort, we used the old-fashioned school "curve" where there are A students, B students, C students, and those who just can't cut it.

Of course, those on the lower end of the scale were never happy with their reviews. And it was difficult to motivate them, especially if they narrowly missed a better raise by an arbitrary cutoff.

While in later years, we used a compensation program that didn't require a certain percentage of cast members in each bucket and used a more esoteric definition of those buckets; whether the cast member was "leading the way" or "exceeding expectations" or simply "meeting expectations," the program still required sorting people by someone's evaluation of performance and growth potential.

Of course, in effect, that was the same thing as the curve. And there was never enough money to reward everyone in the way you'd like.

Companies are eager to promote and reward their star performers, and those are easy discussions to have, but corporate managers can become less enthusiastic about motivating their other team members.

Sometimes, this is the residual effect of the company's restrictive reward and compensation program because managers are not free to award top raises to everyone—again, there isn't enough money designated for that. These managers may find that having some employees perform worse than others becomes an easy way to justify the lower raise they need to give to someone.

"I'm sorry, but I can't give you the same raise as Robert. He is the department's top contributor and deserves the recognition." That works conveniently when you need to validate the system in place.

Companies like to "talk the talk" to their employees. "You are important to us. We respect you. We want the best for you." But those same leaders can fail to "walk the walk" to actually help their employees to become the best they can be. They can fail to motivate.

In that way, lack of development becomes a factor. Obviously, corporate environments are not the same as sports environments, where you win or you are out. Sports teams rely on everyone to contribute as much as they can for the good of the team.

Also, in a corporation, because individuals will likely get annual raises whether the company meets its goals or not, complacency often sets in, and you may not get a 100% effort from all employees.

In sports, the only thing that matters is the results. That *necessitates* an emphasis on development.

There are only fifteen players on an NBA basketball team, so if you are going to give a player a cherished spot on your roster, you want to provide him or her all the tools to succeed: the best equipment, the best practice facilities, best coaches, best doctors and training staff, proven recovery methods, etc.

Your reputation as an organization, and your ability to attract top talent, relies on athletes wanting to play for you.

A nonsports company's environment really shouldn't be much different. Companies choose to have a select number of positions, or head count, as well. So why do many companies have difficulty finding effective ways to develop their staff?

Could it be the bottom line?

In nonsports companies, concerns about meeting or exceeding financial goals always persist—they need to look profitable—and good ideas may be ignored in favor of saving money.

For American corporations in particular, what is implemented and what is not is often a factor of costs.

I once observed an interesting comparison while spending three months living in Hong Kong as part of the Disney task force put in place for the opening of Hong Kong Disneyland in 2005.

For several weeks of that time, I stayed at the Hong Kong Gold Coast Hotel—about five miles from the Disney Resort—in a room that overlooked a small beach adjacent to the complex. This beach stretched about 700 feet in length.

I was always amazed by the number of lifeguards that were on duty for this small area. There were lifeguards in a tower (like you see on California beaches) approximately every 150 to 200 feet. There were three or four more lifeguards on the ground, roaming the sand near the shoreline. Then, finally, there were two more lifeguards in the water itself, watching from a skiff.

I remember thinking this would never happen in the United States despite the advantage it offered for improved safety. In the U.S., someone would think it was too expensive.

Regarding development, it is discouraging to see corporate managers giving up on employees whom they deem as less worthy. They start to give these individuals less difficult, and less fulfilling, projects. They may not consider these team members for valuable classes or learning opportunities or provide a chance to work on assignments where the employee can prove his or her worth. Instead, they lean toward giving the toughest assignments to someone who is more of a "sure thing."

The last move is probably a safety mechanism for the leader because he or she doesn't want the team to fail. But it eliminates an opportunity for others to develop.

And it's not only full-time employees whom companies may overlook or undervalue. Part-time employees often fall into this chasm as well.

I once was urged by my Disney leader at the time not to award one of the few "leading the way" evaluations to a part-time cast member. In his estimation, "you have to work full time to earn that reward."

During the struggles of 2020, the Disney Parks, Experiences and Products division announced in September, as its business tanked due to COVID-19, that they would need to lay off 28,000 cast members. Two months later, as the pandemic carried on, that number was bumped to 32,000, all to be trimmed by the end of March (the first half of the 2021 fiscal year). The predominant portion of those laid off (about two-thirds) were to be part-time cast members.

Now, some of that can be explained by the sheer fact that most of the overall Disney theme park workforce is part time, but that's also due to a policy where the company would rather hire part-time workers in lieu of the more expensive full-time workers, who get costly benefits. Limit the financial exposure by reducing the full-time head count. You don't need to give part-time workers the same guarantees.

Thus, at least at Disney Parks, Experiences and Products, it unfortunately became easy to think of part-time cast members differently and perhaps not as valuable as their longer tenured and better known full-time co-workers.

But in this realm of human development, sports teach us a different lesson. In sports, it's very common for unproven talent to demonstrate their value.

In the world of football, only about thirty high school players a year are evaluated as five-star players—considered the best players in the country—by the various rating services.

Approximately 250–300 players are considered four-star players. These evaluations are used extensively by the schools playing college football, especially the game's biggest programs, to determine whom to pursue and whom to make the offer of a scholarship.

As expected, the most successful college football programs usually gather up the bulk of the four- and five-star high school players.

But it's incredible to see how many guys make it to the NFL who were three-star recruits or less.

Some people marvel at how quarterback Tom Brady went from a sixth-round draft pick to the Greatest of All Time (GOAT) at his position, but it's even more remarkable that Brady was a "no-star" high school player (what these days would be called "unranked"). And so was Ben Roethlisberger of the Pittsburgh Steelers.

Of the thirty-two players selected in the first round of the 2019 NFL draft, eleven were three-star recruits in college, one was a two-star recruit, and three were unranked.

In the 2020 NFL draft first round, ten more three-star recruits were selected as well as one more unranked player.

Remember, I'm talking first round—the thirty-two best players in the country—all of whom would sign multimillion-dollar contracts. All of these individuals, in the span of a few years, developed from being considered negligible to being considered "must haves."

The point is not everyone begins as a star performer. Some people need the right development, or merely the chance to develop. If you are one of these individuals, it should motivate you to know that there are plenty like you who achieve success every year. Are you putting in the proper effort and searching for improvement opportunities or the right environment? Or are you merely accepting the circumstances? Success needs to be earned.

And if you are a nonsports company, are you honestly doing enough to develop your talent? Are you giving up too soon on your employees? Are you committed enough to all of your staff to look past initial impressions and personal biases to provide enough training and opportunities? What are you doing to inspire your young talent?

How many three-star performers are there in the nonsports world who could flourish if given the same opportunities as the known four- and five-star employees?

I'm not saying there aren't forward-thinking companies who understand the value of spending time and money on developing talent for needed roles.

What might that involve? Let's consider a case.

Staff member Jodie may not be abundantly creative, or a valued trainer of up-and-coming performers, but she is really good at being a positive team member and always offers to pitch in where assistance is needed.

Jodie shows up on time, ready to work, and gets along well with others—adding to the team chemistry—and will never say no to an assignment. She possesses a variety of skills, and when she comes across something she doesn't know, she is adept at figuring things out. She has initiative. You can't teach that.

Jodie continually finds a way to make a good contribution and the team is better because of her ongoing efforts.

But if Jodie is not considered a top-tier player by her management team, how will her company evaluate her? Will she be overlooked?

Having a performer like Jodie can be as valuable for a department as a backup "point guard" is for a basketball team.

Given that full-time employees work no more than 239 days a year—after subtracting regular days off, plus a *minimum* of two weeks of vacation, ten holidays, and two sick or personal days off—likely leaves a company with the need for more support. Why not put more emphasis on developing your role players for the sake of the business? To make the company as strong as it can be.

After all, they *are* "the next man up."

AFTER FURTHER REVIEW: *What makes the last two related plays work?*

First, it's identifying the key roles that you need covered by your team in your business. What are the niche roles that can add to the team's success? Do you have capable people filling those roles? Are you underutilizing your three-star players that need more development?

Every sports team knows it takes more than their superstars to win a game. Who are the key role players you can count on? Who will be the unsung heroes that contribute when the game is on the line? Who are the backup players (or part-time staff) itching for an opportunity?

Your business may not look anything like a sports team, but identifying and developing talent will help any business. Spending some money and putting in the effort to find the "diamonds in the rough" will pay off with happier and more engaged employees while establishing a winning reputation for your team.

We all want that street cred!

PLAY #5

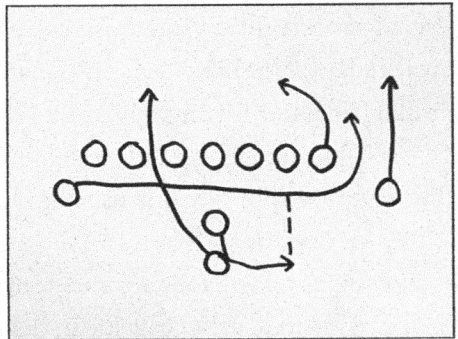

RECOGNIZE A GAME-CHANGING IDEA

It took a long time for Major League Baseball to approve the idea of the *designated hitter.*

The concept was first proposed by Philadelphia Athletics Manager Connie Mack in 1906 because he was frustrated that his pitchers were an easy out.

The idea was considered during the late 1920s by the National League, but not tried.

It resurfaced again in the late 1960s, an era dominated by strong pitching, and finally with the support of colorful Oakland A's owner Charlie Finley, the designated hitter (DH) was introduced in the American League for the 1973 season.

During that year, the American League posted a higher batting average than the National League, a trend that continued through

2019. For the 2020 COVID-19-shortened campaign, the National League agreed to use the DH as a single-season test.

The DH gives baseball managers some strategic advantages, such as the ability to give an everyday player a day off in the field while keeping his bat in the lineup.

There is also an opportunity to rotate players in that role based on who is pitching that day for the other team. This allows the manager to strategically put a left-hand-hitting DH against a right-handed pitcher or a right-hand-hitting DH against a left-handed pitcher.

In the same way that sports teams use big ideas like this to make the game better for the fans and the teams themselves, forward-thinking nonsports companies will take advantage of the talent they have in their organizations to develop new ideas, despite the cost.

It makes sense. Companies know what business issues they have, so why not allow those who know the business best to have an at bat? People are smart. They can figure it out.

The "undeterred niche" is my description of a niche idea that builds momentum to earn its place as a core business for a company.

Once more, Netflix is a good model here.

Netflix began in 1997 as the first online store to rent and sell DVDs, which was a new technology in 1997. Instead of having to drive to a Blockbuster store to get your movies, you could order videos online and they would be mailed to you. A novel concept and nice convenience for the consumer. After a year, Netflix dropped the sales element to focus on rentals.

Then, in 2007, the real idea emerged. Netflix developed a niche business to stream media, in addition to their DVD and Blu-ray rental business (another new technology that year), to deliver movies and TV shows directly to the TVs and computers of consumers. This service offered the extraordinary convenience of "video on demand."

Boom! That's where the business exploded.

In 2013, Netflix entered the content-production business with the popular series *House of Cards.* The company has become a major player in releasing hundreds of pieces of new content every year since—much more than the mainstream Hollywood studios and TV networks produce.

And the payoff has been huge.

As of April 2020, Netflix's streaming service had over 193 million paid subscriptions worldwide. And its business model became the envy of a number of other media companies, which began to develop their own streaming platforms.

On a much smaller and more localized version of the "undeterred niche," we started Broadcast Services at the Disneyland Resort in 1985 as a unique marketing tool.

During the 1980s, while part of Disneyland's publicity department, we did a good job of being the face of the resort in working with print organizations—newspapers and magazines—and for handling interview opportunities for all media, but we didn't create any product for the radio and television outlets interested in covering the Disneyland Resort. (FYI, this was before the commercialization of the internet.).

In 1984, I began producing video news releases (VNRs)—on videotape—to match, in electronic form, the concept of a written press release. At the time, we shot these on 16 mm film, edited them on film Moviolas at Walt Disney Studios in Burbank, mastered them on videotape, and then sent the master to a duplication house to dub hundreds of videotape copies, which we mailed to TV stations.

Obviously, not a quick process.

In 1985, the resort was going to give away General Motors (GM) cars in celebration of its thirtieth birthday, with every 30,000th guest through the main gate winning a car (a Chevrolet, Pontiac, or Buick).

The campaign was the brainchild of Marketing VP Jack Lindquist and required a giant partnership with GM, which Jack wanted to reward with incredible media.

That opened the door for my proposal to build a "broadcast" team at the Disneyland Resort that could capture the moment of each day's car winner, do an interview, then send the footage by satellite to the winner's hometown market for airing on the local news that same day.

Those stories were a boon to our marketing efforts as local stations around the country ran our footage with narrations like, "A Sacramento woman got a great surprise today when, as she passed through the main gate of Disneyland, she won a new Pontiac Firebird!"

Our footage would show the hoopla of confetti and bells going off as the winner was stopped and advised of his or her good luck. Then we would record a soundbite at an outdoor showroom featuring each car model involved in the campaign.

The winner's reaction was always an exceptional PR achievement for the resort. From these VNR satellite feeds, the broadcast team expanded its repertoire to produce electronic press kits, live radio remotes, live television news remotes, and special ride-based camera mounts. We executed all broadcast activities for the resort's major media events—such as maintaining a complete library of resort B-roll and technically producing "live reporter stand-ups" for stations visiting from all over the world.

In all cases, the goal was to implement new ways to add to the resort's overall marketing team effort. Fortunately, resort leadership saw the value in spending the money—millions of dollars a year—to equip this burgeoning department with appropriate labor, capital equipment resources, and operating budget.

Though it wasn't a seamless effort.

Initially, Park Operations didn't like that we were impacting the operation of their attractions and stores and restaurants when we asked for time and space in those environments, sometimes during park operating hours.

Disney parks have always prided themselves on creating a great guest experience, and it was problematic when we requested to shoot in these busy locations for TV commercials, TV specials, TV programming opportunities, still photo campaigns, TV news handout footage and to execute media events and other marketing-based initiatives.

However, with the support of marketing executives like Jack Lindquist, Mark Feary, and Tom Elrod, our friends in Park Operations eventually came to understand that in order to boost attendance to new levels, the resort needed to find new ways to attract guests to the property. So, operations leaders accepted the impact of our projects.

Victory for the Undeterred Niche.

AFTER FURTHER REVIEW: *What makes this play work?*

As the saying goes, necessity is the mother of invention.

A great idea is always waiting in the wings for its chance to become a star. The advent of Netflix streaming proved to be such a phenomenal success that the streaming service world has exploded in the past few years.

A June 26, 2020, story on soda.com identified forty-four streaming services that are now spread across five different categories: On-demand, Free, Niche, Live TV, and Live Sports.

Companies may not always recognize the game-changing idea at first, but great ideas do seem to have a way of being undeterred by individuals without vision and will eventually rise to the surface. When they do, they can not only change the game of sports but the world at large as well.

Keep your eyes and ears open for the game-changing idea that can help you.

PLAY #6

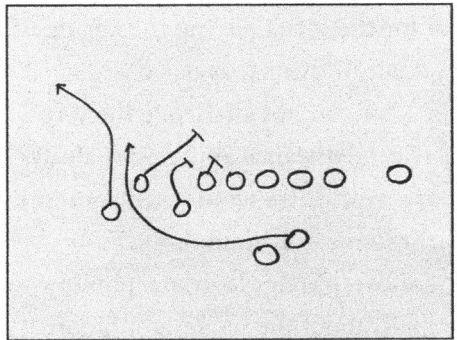

PLAY BY THE RULES

During the COVID-19 pandemic, we, the public, heard constant pleas from healthcare professionals and state leaders alike for all of us to wear a mask.

California was one of the first states to make it mandatory that masks be worn while in public and in places requiring interaction with others.

The point was pretty simple: wearing a mask would not only protect our own personal safety but would work both ways, as we would also be protecting others.

During this stressful time, we needed to be interdependent on each other, since asymptomatic or pre-symptomatic carriers could unknowingly pass along the virus. Scientists noted a newly infected person's contagiousness would peak as much as eighteen hours before they showed any symptoms.

Wearing a mask was seen as the best way to protect ourselves before the availability of a vaccine—advice which was not only simple to abide by but easy to accomplish.

Zlatan Ibrahimovic, a brash but engaging soccer star player, tested positive for COVID-19 while playing for AC Milan when Italy was the hot spot for the virus during the spring of 2020. Later he offered his own advice: "The virus has challenged me, and I won. But you are not Zlatan, do not challenge the virus. Use your head, respect the rules. Social distance and masks, always. We will win."

In the sports world, we would call something as easy, and effective, as wearing a mask a "slam dunk."

It was therefore particularly perplexing to see and hear individuals complain about the request, or ignore it all together, for a variety of reasons that included a theoretical "violation" of their freedoms.

I actually saw video of a Florida woman who rationalized at her local community city council meeting, "I'm not wearing a mask for the same reason I don't wear underwear—things need to breathe."

I admit I had to laugh at that one.

Whether that incident was meant to be humorous or not, there were many situations where disagreements over wearing a mask resulted in nasty arguments or altercations.

Some of this may have been the result of the contentious nature that had permeated itself in the United States. America of 2020 was not a united place to be.

On the contrary, in the sports world, everyone buys into the rules. If you don't, you can't play the game.

When everyone plays by the rules, things are fair for everyone. No one gets an opportunity to cheat.

Even in sports activities where making a mistake can be unintentional, if caught, there comes a price to pay, and all players accept the consequences.

Jump offsides in football, and you will give five free yards to the other team's offense.

Commit a shooting foul in basketball and you give two free throws to the offended player.

As great a baseball player as Pete Rose was, he may never make it to the Hall of Fame because he broke the rules and bet on baseball games.

Barry Bonds, Mark McGwire, Jose Canseco, and Sammy Sosa may not make it to the Hall of Fame for their involvement with performance-enhancing drugs.

Lance Armstrong's cycling legacy will be of someone who won while breaking the rules.

I earlier praised the wisdom of UCLA basketball coach John Wooden.

While he was undoubtedly an honorable and respectful man, his teams also achieved unparalleled success.

During Wooden's tenure, his teams won ten NCAA basketball championships in a twelve-year period, accumulated four perfect 30–0 seasons, and set a record of eighty-eight consecutive victories that will likely never be achieved again in men's basketball.

For quick slices of insight, I still refer to his book *Life Wisdom from Coach Wooden: Inspiring Thoughts from the UCLA Coaching Legend.*

One of my favorite Wooden quotes is this: "I believe we are most likely to succeed when ambition is focused on noble and worthy purposes and outcomes rather than on goals set out of selfishness."

Wooden's success is a great example of good things coming to those who do the right things.

We need those types of role models. We appreciate those who succeed by doing things the right way.

The sanctity of sports relies on those who participate with respect for the principles of the game and who honor the rules.

It might be an incredibly idealistic notion, but wouldn't the world be a better place if we reached for those same goals in everything else?

AFTER FURTHER REVIEW: *What makes this play work?*

Sometimes, when the planet seems to be spinning out of control, the world of sports can not only become our distraction but perhaps offer a better example of how to behave.

Athletes have the pressure to succeed, and the glare of the public wearing on them every day, yet they are keenly aware that playing by the rules is part of the game. It is an absolute.

It's the decorum borne out of rule-making that allows sports, and indeed our world, to function in an orderly and proper way.

It's the etiquette of doing things the right way that embodies the human experience, makes us feel good about the state of affairs, and earns the respect of teammates and opponents alike.

Playing by the rules provides an even playing field for everyone.

PLAY #7

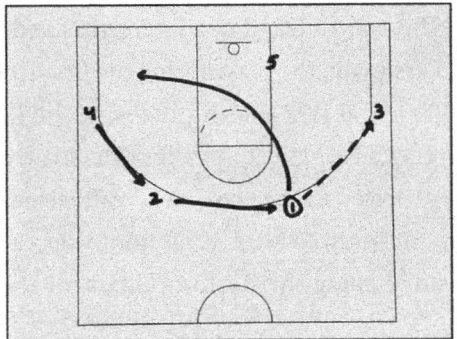

STRIVE TO BE A GOOD TEAMMATE

"God created us to be interdependent. We were not designed
to go through life alone. We become so much more when we
come alongside others — and we make them better, too."

—Coach John Wooden

It is often said that the best players are those who are not only great
contributors themselves but whose presence makes their teammates
better as well.

As a Los Angeles Lakers fan, I watched the 2019–2020 season
with great anticipation as the Lakers added Anthony Davis during
the previous off-season to team up with LeBron James, which many
sports experts described as the best duo in the National Basketball
Association.

While Lakers' team executives hoped to add a third star during
that off-season to create a super team, they were unable to do so

because of timing, finances, and other factors. Instead, they scrambled to put together a team of experienced veterans and capable role players who front-office staff and Lakers fans hoped would be good enough.

Despite it becoming the most unusual year in sports history with the outbreak of the COVID-19 pandemic—leading to a disjointed and shortened NBA schedule—it was interesting and entertaining to watch as the Lakers made the playoffs for the first time in six years.

With LeBron and AD leading the way, the Lakers were the Western Conference's No. 1 seed for the reconstructed NBA playoff picture, and they thrived in the protected Walt Disney World bubble to lead the team to the 2020 NBA Championship—the seventeenth in franchise history, tying the Boston Celtics for the most in NBA history.

Much of the Lakers' success went to three elements: (1) the strong chemistry the team members had built with each other, (2) Coach Frank Vogel's ability to strategically adapt to the circumstances of the game, and (3) LeBron's ability to make those around him better.

Because they were not able to add a star point guard during the off-season, LeBron agreed to take on the unusual role of "point forward" to run the offense and led the league with a career-high 10.2 assists per game.

His strong personality and unique understanding of the game allowed him to essentially be a coach on the floor, and when he was on the floor, the team was particularly good. For his contributions, LeBron earned his fourth NBA Finals MVP Award, becoming the first player to win this award with three different franchises.

LeBron also contributed to great teamwork beyond the basketball floor. He created an organization called More Than a Vote to mobilize a get-out-the-vote effort in Black communities for the 2020 presidential election. He was also a leading voice among NBA players in supporting the Black Lives Matter movement and pushing for social justice.

For his combined athletic and community efforts, LeBron was chosen to be *Time* magazine's Athlete of the Year (2020) and the Associated Press's Male Athlete of the Year in 2020.

During LeBron's career, it's always been remarkable to see how he impacts a game. Instead of looking to use his impressive skills to shoot whenever there is trouble, his first instinct has always been to find the best available scoring option, and if that means someone else, LeBron passes the ball to that teammate.

Now, this is opposite of the kind of "killer instinct" that great players like Michael Jordan and Kobe Bryant were known for, which usually led them to take the most important shots. But LeBron's method is certainly no less successful, and it's also a testimony to the kind of teammate he is.

As discussed in the earlier reference to Alex Caruso, the NBA uses something called Real Plus-Minus (RPM) to measure a player's true individual performance.

There are four elements which measure a player's on-court impact on his team's overall performance:

ORPM: On-court impact on his team's offensive performance.

DRPM: On-court impact on his team's defensive performance.

RPM: On-court impact as measured by point differential.

WINS: On-court impact on total wins.

For the second consecutive year, Giannis Antetokounmpo of the Milwaukee Bucks won the league's Most Valuable Player (MVP) award. Still, it was interesting to see how LeBron measured up as the MVP runner-up.

LeBron ranked first in the league in WINS (Giannis was second), second in the league in RPM (slightly behind Giannis), second in DRPM (Giannis was tenth), and third in ORPM (behind Giannis and James Harden of the Houston Rockets).

That leads to an interesting question for the nonsports business. Instead of solely rewarding employees for the obvious contributions they make, does it also make sense to consider what they do to make the team better?

Certainly, a different way of thinking.

The obviously smart or creative employee may stand out for developing important business ideas, but the great "team player" may be, in the long run, just as important for contributing to a better environment.

That person might actually be the Most Valuable Player.

To use John Wooden's pyramid, how can organizations recognize the individual who works hard, is friendly and cooperative with others, and demonstrates a love for what he or she is doing?

Putting together a group of individuals that actually like each other, and will be there to support each other, can lead to more success than fashioning a team of superstars that all want the ball. Too much internal conflict may make it difficult to build a sense of teamwork, whether on the field or in the office.

Sports have long recognized the value of the "team player." And every team wants that kind of contributor. But companies usually struggle with ways to evaluate, or reward, such performers.

Wouldn't it be nice to find a nonsports workplace example of the "real plus-minus" to reward those who have long been ignored?

AFTER FURTHER REVIEW: *What makes this play work?*

Great teams have their superstars who stand out from other team members and usually earn the biggest accolades. But "team players," those who help others to perform better, are just as cherished in the sports world.

How can those of us in nonsports companies use this example to better recognize the contributions of such individuals, who, in a business environment, may not stand out for their individual achievements and also may not get the kudos they deserve for the way they add value to the team?

As an individual performer, what role can we play to help with the team's success? Perhaps as a mentor to the younger, inexperienced team members? Or possibly for being the team personality that helps others to feel relaxed, included, and more at ease in the workplace?

PLAY #8

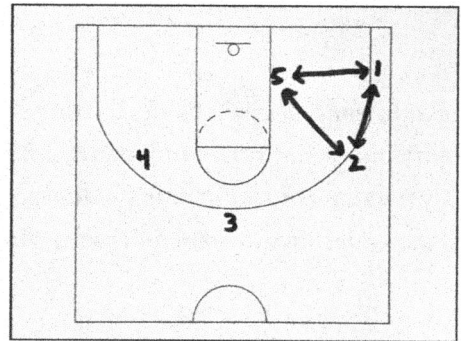

BUILD TEAM CHEMISTRY

A team's general manager always wants to put together the best collection of talent possible. He or she will build their teams with consideration for what they already have, and what they believe is lacking.

"We are one superstar short . . . We need another three-point shooting specialist . . . We've got to find a relief pitcher who can be our closer . . . We need a lockdown corner for our defensive secondary."

For the 2019–2020 NBA season, the Los Angeles Clippers put together a deep and talented roster that many NBA experts picked to win the championship.

Adding to a solid team that had a respected coach (Doc Rivers), the Clippers signed two superstars—two-time Finals MVP Kawhi Leonard and prolific forward Paul George. They were considered to be two of the ten best players in the league.

Leonard and George were surrounded by the best bench in the league, including Lou Williams, the winner of three NBA Sixth Man of the Year Awards, and Montrezl Harrell, who became the winner of the Sixth Man of the Year Award in 2020.

Prior to the trade deadline, the Clippers also added Marcus Morris, perhaps the best player on the New York Knicks team, and Reggie Jackson, a capable guard from the Oklahoma City Thunder.

The Clippers entered the Western Conference Semi-Finals as the undisputed favorite against a scrappy Denver Nuggets team. The Clippers' goal was to advance to the Western Conference Finals for the first time in team history, and they looked well on their way with an overwhelming three games to one lead.

Then it all fell apart.

The Nuggets had fought back from a 3–1 deficit in their previous series against the Utah Jazz, and for the final three games of this series, they played incredible second halves during which they routed the Clippers by scores of 67–49, 64–35, and 50–33 respectively.

While young, the Nuggets played loose, with efficiency and energy, and they had fun. They are a group of guys who like each other and play as a team.

On the other hand, the Clippers, while finishing as the No. 2 seed in the Western Conference, had a bumpy season and had difficulty all along in developing team chemistry.

Paul George had a late start to the season as he recovered from an injury. Kawhi Leonard was getting planned days off for "load management" as Doc Rivers tried to assure Kawhi's freshness for the post-season.

Once they arrived in Orlando for the NBA playoffs, the Clippers were late in getting all their players together.

Lou Williams left the bubble to go to a wedding, and because of a trip to a strip bar for dinner, he was forced to quarantine for ten days upon his return.

Montrezl Harrell and Patrick Beverley also left the bubble to attend to medical emergencies. Harrell was gone for a month.

Ivica Zubac, the starting center, and Landry Shamet, a reserve guard, were late arrivals to Orlando as well, as they recovered at home from the COVID-19 virus. The Clippers hoped they had the talent to overcome those negatives during the playoffs, but the lack of team cohesiveness proved to be an issue.

As Williams said to the media after the final game, "We did have championship expectations and we had the talent to do it. I don't think we had the chemistry to do it, and it showed."

As a casualty of the circumstance, coach Doc Rivers lost his job.

This, of course, is not the first time a talented team did not win it all. But it is yet another example of the importance of team chemistry and finding the right formula for success.

Building a great sports team is tricky. There needs to be a delicate mix of headliners with willing and capable supporting cast— all willing to do whatever it takes to work in unity and all contributing their unique pieces to an intricate puzzle.

It's kind of like a recipe. If you have too much of one ingredient and too little of another, or if you don't cook it properly, it's not going to have the great taste you, as the chef, anticipated.

In the nonsports workplace, seemingly innocent changes can impact team chemistry. One person retires and is replaced by someone with less experience and skill.

A department promotion puts the rewarded individual into a position to interact with other team members differently than before and perhaps without the same success.

One co-worker, eager to prove oneself, may encroach on another's area of responsibility, causing a disintegration of rapport and trust.

The basic concept of team chemistry may be something athletes think more about than nonsports organizations.

For sure, competition to advance in the corporate workplace depends on showing one's worth and standing out. The overall "team" goal likely isn't emphasized the same way as in sports—a corporate manager usually doesn't think that way and may not have a compelling vision to convey.

And the variables are, to put it simply, more varied. Differences in age. A mixture of men and women. Different educational and business experience (backgrounds). Different goals. In a phrase, there are more disjointed parts.

I used to think that it was more important to hire a new team member who could mesh well with the existing team than it was to find the most experienced or knowledgeable individual.

We could always train someone how to do the job, but an ill-placed personality would be like trying to make a football wide receiver out of a short, slow player with bad hands. A bad fit.

In the true spirit of sports achievement, I would surmise the most successful nonsports environments are those where the individuals earnestly work "together" and complement each other.

During my years at Disney, we had many successful leaders who ran such teams. Usually, it began with finding team members who wanted to be in the environment. Those who sought out Disney employment and were motivated to be there, much like an athlete who seeks a professional sports career.

It was also important that the team leader be adept at expressing his or her vision so all team members could buy into the mission at hand.

When everyone knows the process, it is easier to work in unison.

Also, people want to feel important and needed. And conveying that to team members is essential for team morale.

Disney Pixie Dust was achieved when our team members realized how special their environment truly was and then demonstrated a commitment to keeping it special.

With the combined efforts of *all* team members, we could not only achieve success but also enjoy the ride getting there.

AFTER FURTHER REVIEW: *What makes this play work?*

Sports teams have the advantage of a single identity. A group of individuals all poised to pursue the same goal.

But with a good leader who can clearly express and sell the team's vision, and team members who are invested in the mission, a business-world team can find a unity of purpose that is just as compelling.

Find the right situation for yourself, determine how you can contribute or lead, and be a positive factor in achieving team cohesiveness.

PLAY #9

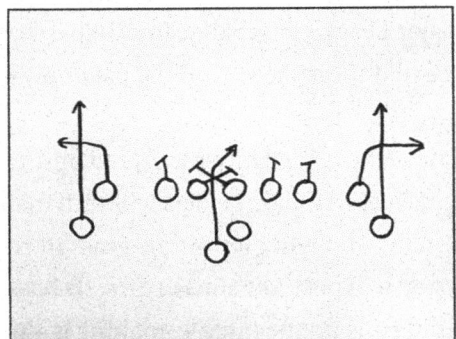

USE YOUR ADVANTAGES

Play your game. Play to your strengths.

There is no rule in sports that says you have to use less successful methods to be fair to the other team.

While good sportsmanship is a cherished quality for athletes to possess, the games are played to be won, not tied or lost. Good sports teams will play to their strengths.

A football team that is piling up yards, first downs, and touchdowns by running the ball is going to continue to run the ball.

As we would expect to hear the coach say to his players in that situation: "We're going to continue to run that play until they prove they can stop it."

A basketball team that has an advantage with bigger, taller players is going to look to score in the paint—where points are easier to come by than with the three-point shot. And if a team is under-sized, they are going to shoot as many three-point shots as they can hoist up, like the 2019–2020 Houston Rockets, especially after choosing to build a smaller, quicker team around James Harden, a great outside shooter.

In recent years, metrics or data have been used to great advantage by Major League Baseball teams. In baseball, pretty much everything is charted these days. And the data now dictate how the game is played.

If you know a left-handed hitter will predominantly put the ball in play to the right side, all four infielders will shift that way, including the second baseman, who will play on the grass in right field.

The shortstop will position himself directly behind second base to stop any ground balls up the middle, making it almost impossible to get a ground ball through the infield unless the hitter can overcome his tendencies and hit the ball to the left side.

During the 2020 World Series, the Tampa Bay Rays played four outfielders for five different Los Angeles Dodgers players who were known as fly ball hitters. The purpose of this strategy was to attempt to eliminate any doubles that would have been hit into the left-field or right-field alleys.

For those situations, the Rays looked like they were playing a softball game.

In the sixth and final game of the World Series, Rays manager Kevin Cash relied on metrics to take out his best pitcher, Blake Snell, after Snell had tossed five and 1/3 innings of masterful baseball in which he struck out nine Los Angeles Dodgers players and only gave up one run.

The theory here was that most starting pitchers see a jump in opposing team's batting average the third time through the order as batters adapt to the pitches being thrown. When Dodgers' catcher Austin Barnes got a hit in the sixth inning, Snell was removed.

Up to that point, the Dodgers' first four hitters had gone 0-for-8 at the plate, with seven strikeouts. As it turned out, the change of pitchers put the Rays on the wrong side of the data.

Mookie Betts, an exceptional player and the Dodgers' next hitter, was now facing Nick Anderson, a right-handed pitcher. Snell is left-handed and during the course of the season, Betts had struggled against left-handed pitchers. But he had hit one hundred points higher against right-handed pitchers, including belting all sixteen of his home runs against righties, and Anderson had given up a run in each of his previous five outings.

So, the Rays' effort to play the metrics actually parlayed into an advantage for the Dodgers.

Sure enough, Betts laced a double to left field with Barnes stopping at third base. Barnes scored when Anderson threw a wild pitch, and Betts used his speed to score the go-ahead run when Corey Seager hit a ground ball to first base.

After Betts hit a home run in the eighth inning to give the Dodgers a 3–1 lead, relief pitcher Julio Urias put the Rays away to give the Dodgers their first World Series title in thirty-two years, and the seventh in franchise history.

The Dodgers' advantage all year long had been their tremendous power, timely two-out hitting, speed, pitching, and defense. And all of those elements played a role in their successful post-season run.

For those of us who aren't the Dodgers, we see groups and individuals often suffer when trying to be something they are not. An individual may have a great desire to be an actor or singer or corporate leader but lack the ideal skills to succeed. I was never going to be another Sandy Koufax.

Humans seek esteem. We feel good with positive feedback but feel bad with negative feedback.

People obtain esteem in three different ways: self-esteem for situations where we know we have put in the proper effort, esteem from others who respect what we have achieved, and pseudo-esteem for things we are credited for simply because of our reputation.

Of the three, self-esteem is the most important. It is the voice of our internal audience that evaluates our efforts. A good effort gets a nod of approval, but a poor effort will get internal criticism. The internal audience only cares about effort, not results.

Using the evaluation powers of our self-esteem, and factoring in the esteem of others (or lack of it if we aren't very good at an endeavor), is valuable in telling us if we are in the right job or right situation—or need to do better or possibly move on to something else that is a better fit.

As a result, we all know what our strengths and weaknesses are. If we find ourselves in a job where the required skills are the ones we don't have, we will likely do the work without confidence or enthusiasm or enjoyment. Deep down, we know the situation is not right—something is amiss.

But we will surely get more base hits, or achieve more personal success in whatever we attempt, if we build our efforts around our strengths.

Fortunately, not all advantages need to be big. Some can be subtle. I have a friend who possesses a great sense of humor. I have always admired people with a terrific sense of humor.

Even during times of huge personal stress, I am amazed how this friend is able to find a nugget of humor to lighten up the situation and make others feel better.

In that time of need, when she knows things appear shaky, she plays to her strengths and helps those around her to laugh.

I am so glad she does.

AFTER FURTHER REVIEW: *What makes this play work?*

Accomplished teams find success by taking advantage of tactics they do well. Trying to simulate the tactics of other successful teams would be fruitless if your team's strengths are different.

You know the old saying: a tiger can't change its stripes.

Be on the lookout for circumstances that may change the advantages either for you or against you. Remember what happened to the Tampa Bay Rays when they took out their best pitcher, Blake Snell, and the advantages shifted to the Los Angeles Dodgers.

As an individual, remember, we know what we are good at, and what is simply an unobtainable dream.

Being honest with ourselves will keep us on the right track to engage in life in ways we can be successful.

PLAY #10

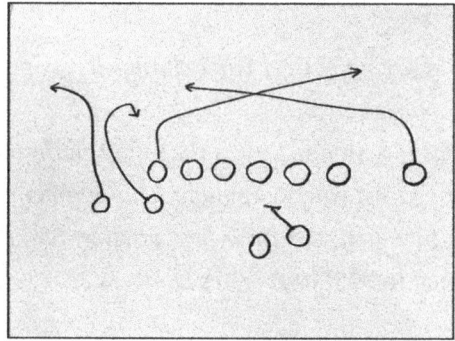

DEVELOP A WINNING ATTITUDE

After Game 3 of the 2020 NBA Western Conference Semifinals against the Houston Rockets in which he scored thirty-six points and took over first place for the most career wins in playoffs history, LeBron James said:

"I just think that when you've been in the process and you've been building your mind, your body, and your soul for the postseason, no matter the circumstances, then you're going to rise. Now that doesn't mean you're always gonna play well. That doesn't mean you're gonna win. But you can leave the game and sleep okay at night if you lose."

Once again, it's the process.

Winning athletes develop a winning attitude. It's part of the drive that keeps them going when the going gets tough.

In the 2003 movie based on the real-life racehorse Seabiscuit, Jockey Red Pollard, played by Tobey Maguire, is preparing to participate in the biggest race of his career—a match race against the vaunted Triple Crown winner War Admiral—when Pollard suffers a broken leg while trying to help an old friend.

This was a race that Seabiscuit's owner, Charles Howard, had been campaigning for months to arrange. And it had garnered national interest for pitting a compelling David-versus-Goliath scenario during a time when the country was trying to rebound from the Great Depression of 1929, and looking for feel-good moments.

Because Seabiscuit was undersized, walked with a slight limp, and had little success early in his career, he was a decided underdog for this race.

In the movie, after the injury, Red advises Mr. Howard to call George Woolf to take his place. Woolf was Red's good friend and was acknowledged as the best jockey in the world at the time. As the movie aptly described, it was like calling Babe Ruth to the plate to be a pinch hitter.

In a pre-race encounter in his hospital room, Red is shown to be counseling Woolf about Seabiscuit's tendencies. He says he expects Seabiscuit will get out quickly and take the lead, and advises Woolf to hold that lead until they get to the backstretch. Then Red tells Woolf to let War Admiral catch up.

Woolf is surprised at that suggestion, as in "Why stop our momentum?" What athlete would suggest that? Momentum is what every team or individual wants during a sporting event.

"Just hold him through that final turn and let him get a good look at the Admiral," Red says. "Then let him go. It's not in his feet, Georgie," Red adds as he taps his chest. "It's right here."

When that moment comes in the race, it's the best part of the movie for me.

There is an exhilaration that comes from winning. A great feeling from knowing you've encountered a difficult challenge, put everything into your effort, and came out on top.

The tougher the challenge, the better it feels. Nobody proves anything by accomplishing something that's easy to do.

The best athletes want the toughest road to a championship.

And the best athletes nurture and refine a winning attitude that becomes part of their persona to take on the most difficult tasks and the hardest challenges, to carry themselves to success.

One of the more incredible, recent examples of winning attitude involved Alex Smith, the quarterback of the Washington Football Team (previously the Washington Redskins), and his recovery from an "open" fracture which occurred on November 18, 2018, in a game against the Houston Texans.

Throughout his career, Alex had displayed a winner's DNA. He was the first overall pick of the 2005 NFL draft by the San Francisco 49ers after a stellar college career at the University of Utah, where he compiled a 21–1 record as a starter, playing for coach Urban Meyer.

His first few years in San Francisco were difficult, but then, in 2011, Alex led the 49ers to their first National Football Conference (NFC) title and playoff victory since 2002, along with their first NFC Championship Game appearance since 1997.

In 2012, a concussion caused Alex to lose his job to Colin Kaepernick and, in 2013, he was traded to the Kansas City Chiefs, whom he led to a 9–0 start and a playoff berth.

In 2015, he led the Chiefs to an eleven-game winning streak and their first playoff win since 1993.

In 2017, the Chiefs drafted the immensely talented Patrick Mahomes and, in 2018, Smith was traded to the Redskins. He had the team in first place at 6–3 when that horrendous broken leg incident occurred and took Smith down a path that required a prodigious level of physical and mental fortitude. The kind of unwavering attitude that winners develop.

Alex's leg was broken so badly that he was taken directly to the hospital for surgery, still wearing his uniform, with a smattering of dirt and grass, a piece of his sock, plus bacteria from the field entering the puncture wound.

What appeared like a routine surgery turned into a nightmare that nearly took Alex's life.

A few days after the surgery, rare flesh-eating disease (necrotizing fasciitis) began to destroy the tissue in Alex's right leg. Damaged skin turned black and became unsalvageable, and the bacteria was infecting his soft tissue and leg muscle as well. He began experiencing sepsis, a life-threatening condition.

Alex's wife, Elizabeth, inquired about having Alex's leg amputated to terminate the spread if that would save his life, but the response from the team doctor was, "Our first priority is to save his life. And then we're going to do our best to save his leg. And anything beyond that is a miracle."

Doctors performed a debridement eight times—a surgical procedure to remove skin, tissue, and muscle to eliminate infection—leaving Alex's tibia completely exposed. His right leg was missing everything except for the bone from the knee to the ankle and side to side. It had to be rebuilt with muscle and tissue from his other leg.

When given the options and made aware of the challenges, including that the muscle transfer might not be successful, meaning his injured leg might have to be amputated anyway and his remaining leg would now be weakened, Alex responded with the kind of determination of a successful athlete. He said, "Let's do it. Let's go."

During another display of incredible attitude, after a surgery following the period when doctors were still concerned about saving his life, Alex said to Elizabeth, "Do you know how many people would love to trade positions with me? Millions of people would love to be here where I am right now. Do you know the life we live and the blessings we have? And we can't take it for granted, not even for a minute. Perspective."

Because his injury had transcended a normal sports injury into the kind of damage seen by members of the military who sustain blast trauma, he was able to obtain permission to get treatment at a military rehab center in San Antonio, Texas, called the Center for the Intrepid.

This was a positive experience for Alex, and he began to call the day of his injury "Alive Day," which is what military members call the day they survive a traumatic injury.

He observed soldiers doing things for their own recoveries that athletes never have to do, and he was inspired. Alex began to think beyond his survival and recovery to once again believe that football could be part of his life again.

And on November 15, 2020, after seventeen surgeries and twenty months of recovery, Alex Smith started again in a game for the Washington Football Team. A game it won. He went on to earn the NFL's Comeback Player of the Year award for 2020, before announcing his retirement in April 2021.

While few of us will encounter the kind of life-threatening tumult that Alex Smith lived through, his toughness and resolve are wonderful examples of how humans can endure even the most difficult conflicts with a positive attitude, a winning attitude.

From the 2018 season to the end of the 2020 season, Alex Smith was 11–5 as Washington's quarterback. All others who played quarterback for the team during that time were 6–26.

In the nonsports world, such as in an office of disparate personalities, you don't find the warrior personalities of athletes or soldiers but, overall, we are not dealing with the same challenges for survival either.

It may be difficult to get everyone in your real-world environment—where you have an eclectic mix of men and women, young and old, experienced and new hires, leaders and contributors—to hold their egos in check for the pursuit of a single-purpose operation.

There may also be circumstances where disagreeable personalities make it difficult to build that great team chemistry, fomenting a chaos instead, which may dishearten the more emotional individuals who can struggle in an unsettled environment. But, as we all know, attitude is of our own choosing.

In the nonsports world, perhaps the winning attitude is simply buying into the philosophy of being a "team player?" In trying to do what is best for the team, despite the sacrifices it may personally require of us.

It's not always easy to give of yourself when you see others who are not putting the same effort. But I would always want a player like that on my team—someone who is respectful, unselfish, and committed to the cause. That's my kind of winning attitude.

AFTER FURTHER REVIEW: *What makes this play work?*

Winners have winning attitudes that push them to succeed.

Not much in life is accomplished without the proper motivation. The desire to be good at our job, and to be successful, is a great motivator. The more difficult the task, the better it feels to win.

In the business world, where it's more difficult to get everyone on the same page, attitude is likely more important than intelligence. And a winning attitude can simply start with being a positive influence as well as having a willingness to give of oneself for the sake of the group's chance to prosper. Choosing a course of respect, unselfishness, and commitment to the mission will earn a great reputation for you.

PLAY #11

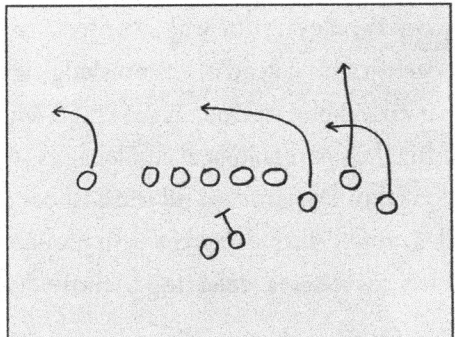

COMPETITION MAKES YOU BETTER

The late Alex Trebek, the esteemed host of the long-running TV show *Jeopardy!* was doing an interview a few years ago when he was asked about the success of his show. His response:

"America is a very competitive society. 'I can throw the ball farther than you can. I can run faster than you. I can do better on *Jeopardy!* than you.' 'Okay, let's see.'"

Somewhere over the last few decades, parents began to be afraid of psychologically hurting the development of their kids by putting them through sporting experiences where they could lose.

They argued that losing could create a negative psychological foundation for impressionable individuals who don't have the mental toughness of an adult.

Schools and sports leagues were pressured to employ alternate ways to reward kids for their participation in sports activities; that is, other than recognizing the winners.

Convinced schools and sports leagues decided not to award special accolades to youth teams that won. In some cases, games were not even scored and everyone was awarded a trophy, or given a "participation" certificate, instead of acknowledging the best team.

Evolutionary psychologist Doug Lisle, Ph.D., who is particularly astute in explaining life's psychological challenges as the originator of a website called Esteem Dynamics, and the co-host of an insightful podcast called *Beat Your Genes*, disagrees with the efforts he describes as "trauma pandering." That is, deferring to individuals who believe losing does harm.

Dr. Lisle calls this the "Bruised Banana Theory." During a personal interview with me he described it this way:

"Children are like bananas in the grocery store. If you pick up bananas and squeeze them a bit you know that when you take them home and pull back the peel you will notice they are bruised a bit, making them less attractive and less appealing.

"Every tiny bump to your kids in their life is going to bruise them a bit. Some parents think their job is to shield their kids from these bruises so someday, when they try to compete in the adult world, and someone pulls back the peel, there will be no bruises. But this is a ludicrous idea.

"A great quote from the movie *Hard Times* is that 'the next best thing to playing and winning is playing and losing.' In fact, it's a huge mistake to believe that your children, in being disappointed by loss, will incur any damage at all. It's a natural part of the growth process to test our abilities, and sometimes we surprise ourselves with the positive, and sometimes we get disappointed in the negative. That, however, in no way damages human motivation."

The process of shielding our kids—or even ourselves—from competition falls into a practice known as "competitive avoidance."

Competitive avoidance describes the various ways people will latch on to any excuse to avoid fair competition.

While this practice is widely seen in the everyday world, and you may have witnessed it yourself as a method your co-workers or acquaintances have used to avoid the possibility of rejection or defeat, it is *not* a part of the cost–benefit analysis that athletes use.

Athletes compete as a matter of livelihood.

According to Dr. Lisle from one of the *Beat Your Genes* podcasts: "The only place confidence comes from is from the internal observation of the improvement of your body or mind. You've got to play and lose. Then you correct, learn, and grow.

"The notion you should get through life with minimal discomfort is wrong. The notion that losing reduces self-confidence is ridiculous. Losing *should* suck. The process of watching yourself improve is what resilience is all about. That's the secret sauce.

"If we put in a full effort and lose, we still get self-esteem. That is independent of outcome."

To use an old sports axiom, it really is how you play the game that matters the most. Winning or losing is secondary.

In professional sports, Pete Carroll, current coach of the Seattle Seahawks and previous coach of the USC Trojans football team from 2001 to 2009, has achieved great success by embracing competition on the practice field.

Carroll lives by a philosophy of "iron sharpening iron."

In other words, during practice, instead of thinking of the man playing opposite you as someone you want to beat to prove your value, think how much better it is for the team as a whole if, during your practice time, you are helping each other to improve?

In that case, you are making each other better.

Another practice ritual that Carroll refined at USC was something he called "Competition Tuesdays," where everyone competed for a starting role in that week's game.

This was another "win-win" situation where the competition made sure there was no complacency among the starters, while also giving eager backups a chance to get valuable repetitions to prove themselves.

The bottom line, of course, is that competition is not something to be feared. Challenges keep us alert and on course to be better students, employees, teammates, and people.

The popular TV series *The Big Bang Theory*, which follows the quirky lives of a group of scientists who are friends, actually made a unique foray into the world of sports during season twelve, episode ten.

That episode finds Sheldon, who thought of himself as a scientific superstar, getting the alarming news that one of his cherished theories was disproven by a team of Russian scientists.

The revelation sends perfectionist Sheldon into a spiraling funk which his wife, Amy, tries to turn around, but even with the aid of their friends, she can't.

Amy discovers Sheldon's "emergency" videotape, which he recorded as a kid, to be used as a sort of anti-venom (aka pep talk) in the event a situation like this ever occurred.

Unfortunately, the key portion of this video was taped over by Sheldon's father, a high school football coach, to record one of his games. Thus, Sheldon becomes even more distressed with the realization that his cherished message has been carelessly erased.

At the depth of Sheldon's depression, he finds Amy still trying to find his childhood speech on the videotape, but instead, she discovers a surprising halftime speech by Sheldon's dad.

"I know we're down and probably not going to win this," his dad tells his team. "We're *definitely* not going to win this! We're not going to quit either. But if we do lose, that doesn't make you losers. You learn as much by failing as you do from success. Maybe more. So, you can go out there the next half feeling sorry for yourself or go out and give them hell."

Of course, in true Hollywood fashion, the speech revives Sheldon, who responds philosophically, "I've been feeling like the game is over, but it's only halftime, and there's a lot more physics to play."

Amy is happy to see Sheldon's spirit return. "Is that your first sports metaphor?"

He says, "Yes, and I think it's a home run." (We all appreciate a good joke during poignant moments like that, don't we?)

And it's true; whether we employ mixed metaphors or not, competition is definitely a valued learning experience. And it makes us better if we give it a chance.

We've all heard the metaphor, "When the going gets tough, the tough get going."

Again, this is a concept that athletes live by. But in the real world, I've seen lots of situations where this resolve is lacking and where an individual could benefit from the positive examples generated in athletics.

I actually know someone who has a history of giving up once an endeavor gets too difficult. I've seen it cause this person to leave a job. To give up on a personal relationship. To abdicate responsibility. And even to doubt, overall, that he has the tools to be successful in this ultracompetitive world.

This individual believes if the circumstances don't align then that must be a sign to move on. The reality is, life doesn't make it easy on us. Life is a continual competitive process. We are always competing with others for the same resources.

I think there is an ethos that athletes have, where a type of adrenaline kicks in during difficult times to push themselves forward.

They wouldn't consider abandoning something worthwhile without first putting in their best effort to accomplish it.

Ultimately, all of us can gain by thinking that way.

AFTER FURTHER REVIEW: *What makes this play work?*

Contrary to some philosophical beliefs, we should not be afraid of competition for either ourselves or our kids.

Engaging in competition and failing is a positive experience, as it is part of getting better as an individual.

When we lose, we learn to correct our actions and grow. If we put in a full effort and lose, we still get self-esteem. That is independent of outcome.

Teams now encourage heated internal competition as a means to provoke personal development. In practice, when an offensive lineman and defensive lineman are physically challenging each other, they are actually helping each other to improve.

The process of watching ourselves improve is what resiliency is all about. Don't allow fear to prompt you to abandon your goals.

Don't fall into the trap of competitive avoidance.

PLAY #12

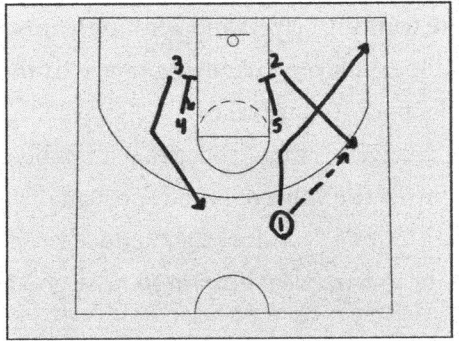

WHY WE HAVE A DESIRE TO WIN

America thinks of itself as a nation of winners, and Americans want to win in every way possible:

- Through the ideology and values our nation was founded upon.
- Through the political opinions we espouse.
- Through the ideas we share with the world.
- Through the economy with which we build our wealth.
- Through the businesses we own.
- Through the children we raise.
- Through the wars we fight.
- Through the groups and organizations we decide to support.
- Through the teams we choose to follow.

Winning makes us happy. Winning makes us feel accomplished. Winning makes us feel important.

Winners are what we want to be.

Winning is revered, rewarded, sought, and—for those who have done it—honored and respected.

It is a common practice, and accepted accolade, for a U.S.-based championship team to be invited to the White House to be honored.

Fans adore winning players and winning teams, especially their local teams and local players that bring honor to the city, and who help fans to feel a part of that success.

Winning receives so much focus that it has become important to teach our children the value of "good sportsmanship" so they can exhibit the qualities of a "good winner" or a "graceful loser." After all, while we want to win, we still want to raise good human beings as well.

Perhaps in no other country are sports such an integral part of the fabric of society than in the United States, where an incredible number of sports are taught, played, followed, adored, attended, and broadcast.

The country is steeped in a sports mindset. It's no surprise, then, to see the lasting impact of sports moments.

In a lot of ways, sports are society's accepted version of war.

It's a fight for superiority without the lethal weapons.

Our local heroes go to battle, and with victory, we feel a community sense of pride. Psychologically, whenever a group is divided into two smaller groups, a sense of favoritism is created—"us" against "them."

In wars, those groups are nations fighting for resources—sometimes tangible items like property, wealth, and women—and, sometimes, for more idyllic values, like freedom.

Those who win acquire wealth, respect, and notoriety.

The same happens in sports. The fans of winning sports teams earn the same sense of pride and invincibility. They enjoy the prestige of being on top.

For some, it becomes a part of their soul and defines who they are.

When I was going to USC in the 1970s, the Trojans football team, a recognized college football powerhouse, went to the Rose Bowl each of the final three years I was a student and won college football national championships in 1972 and 1974. The '72 squad, which had a 12–0 record, has been recognized as one of the greatest teams in college football history.

I felt I was important, simply for being part of that environment. I felt like a winner, too, especially during my last semester when I was editor of the *Daily Trojan* student newspaper. And when I graduated, I felt like USC's sports prowess put additional shine on my diploma.

USC appeared in three more Rose Bowls in the '70s, following my graduation, and won another national championship. And over the years, USC has won more Rose Bowls than any other school.

That success became a part of my own personality. It was interesting, then, what happened when the Trojans football team hit a down cycle in the 1990s. After appearing in the Rose Bowl six times during the '70s decade, USC, while not as dominant in the '80s, still earned four Rose Bowl appearances.

But in the 1990s, the program was nothing more than mediocre and only earned one trip.

For the predominant part of that decade, the team wasn't very good.

I remember that lack of accomplishment sometimes affecting my personal confidence, and definitely my mood, especially during college football season.

One day, I was in a bookstore when I heard a man in the next aisle commiserating about the state of USC football. As I looked over the stack of books to see if this was someone I knew, he noticed me staring at him and stopped talking. I said to him, "Are you a USC football fan?"

He replied, "Yes, do you want to kick me while I'm down?"

And after sharing a laugh, I responded with empathy, "So am I and I know exactly what you mean. What happened to us? We used to be somebody!"

We went on to talk about the situation for another ten minutes, like two war buddies sharing battle stories, and I felt really good I wasn't alone in my misery. I was understood.

Psychologist Dr. Doug Lisle says the emotions involved here are really very evolutionary in nature, going back to stone-age times when people lived in small tribes.

During my interview with him, Dr. Lisle explained it like this: "If you were in a tribe that was dominant, that would impact your confidence in several ways, not only in your survival, but in your assessment of resources you had rights to. Being dominant would make you more assertive and convince you the time was right to raid the village across the river for their resources.

"Warfare is biologically a human nature. And it is only in males. We don't know of any other species that goes to war other than humans and chimpanzees. But men are conditional hawks. They are very interested in warfare if they have a decided advantage. But only if they have a big advantage. Otherwise, the costs are too high."

That rationalizes the change in behavior I experienced when the USC football team with which I identified lost its luster, creating anxiety about its lack of success. I became less confident, and in no mood to wave the SC banner to display those genes. Or to boast about our circumstances.

The chain of psychological events goes from perception to calculation to emotion to behavior. When we see our tribe win, we calculate that winning will increase our influence over our local landscape, making us better off. And when we are better off, we feel good and happy and confident and assertive. And when we are assertive, we want to claim our resources. But when we are in a down cycle, we want to lay low.

Dr. Lisle stated that is what happens to teams like the Cleveland Cavaliers, who were flying high when LeBron James rejoined the team for the 2014-2015 season, leading it to four straight NBA Finals appearances, including an NBA championship during the 2015-2016 season. But then he left the franchise for the Los Angeles Lakers after the 2017-2018 season.

Cleveland's advantages dissipated with that move and the Cavaliers became one of the worst teams in the league. The franchise's attendance figures tell the story. Before LeBron's 2014 arrival, Cleveland was sixteenth in the league in total attendance. During his four years with the team, the Cavs sold out every game and ranked second in the league in total attendance. But the team fell to eighth in attendance following LeBron's 2018 departure as enthusiasm waned, and returned to pre-LeBron territory at seventeenth in the league for the 2019-2020 season.

"People live their lives trying to manage the oppressions of the existing social environment," Dr. Lisle said. "So, it makes sense as a sports fan when you are invited into a coalition of a team that's winning. The nervous system is sensitive about being in a position of advantage. That generates excitement.

"Men look at athletes as a warfare coalition member. And will gauge whether they are personally going to be able to gain from that member's contributions as a member of the pack."

Dr. Lisle did point out there are two noteworthy elements that separate warfare from sports. One is an independent process called a "display." These displays have "fitness indicators."

"Fitness indicators will show variances to the opposite sex," Dr. Lisle outlined. "Females look at how physically different men are to them — muscles, deepness of their voice, body shape. These indicators are generated by genes and are like advertising slogans in what they say about that individual.

"However, sports is a method for keeping the challenges even. Everyone shoots at a basket that is 10 feet off the floor. And the rules create an equality so that the variance comes from the quality of an athlete's fitness indicators.

"Also, playing sports showcases one's genetic quality. And if you are a member of a tribe that wins — going back to stone-age thinking — that would mean you share the genes of the person that did the winning, which means their greatness becomes a fitness indicator for you. That's why you want to wear Michael Jordan's jersey. It's not just you are like Mike; you are RELATED to him!"

This brings us to both a benefit and a target of our success—the attainment of status. When a team wins a championship it acquires the dividend of status which we, as individuals, also acquire from our own competitive victories: the school honor roll, the big promotion at work, the prestigious new client, the special recognition for a noteworthy accomplishment, etc.

Status is like the pursuit of the Holy Grail. Everyone wants it. And no one wants to give it up. We want to build or maintain status while our competitors want to wrest it from us.

We may see more personal and team victories as part of an organization (or tribe) that is built for success, but sometimes the status we covet may be beyond our personal control.

Dr. Lisle summarized the vagaries we experience in life this way:

"Life is a process of oscillating good and bad fortune. Those with whom we compete don't innately have any advantages over us. Nor do they have any greater liabilities.

"The average mental state of the average human is neither one of advantage nor disadvantage. It's our individual nervous systems that are sensitive to the observation of what is happening around us."

So, in practice, it would be wise, and probably a lot less stressful, for us to recognize that while winning is fun, and should be enjoyed, playing the game and living our lives in the proper perspective would be valuable.

That is, realize, as winners, we will have our own downtimes too and when that happens, we just need to ride out that roller coaster.

Hopefully, without too much angst.

AFTER FURTHER REVIEW: *What makes this play work?*

As we learned from the previous chapter, engaging in competition teaches us valuable lessons.

One of those lessons is that we're not going to win 100% of the time. For that reason, going through life's trials and tribulations and coming out successful becomes a real ego boost for us.

It builds confidence for us and makes us feel accomplished, important, and assertive. The more we are part of something successful, the more important we feel. But the harder we may fall if that success is suddenly halted.

So, we need to be aware of the "ego trap"—pursuing success at all costs—and, instead, realize that while winning is fun, and should be enjoyed, playing the game (and living your life) with the right set of principles, and putting them in the proper perspective, is even more of a win in the long run.

Do the best you can in your endeavors, and if that leads to a win, celebrate your success. But don't let a loss defeat you. Use it to work on improvements toward your next "up cycle."

PLAY #13

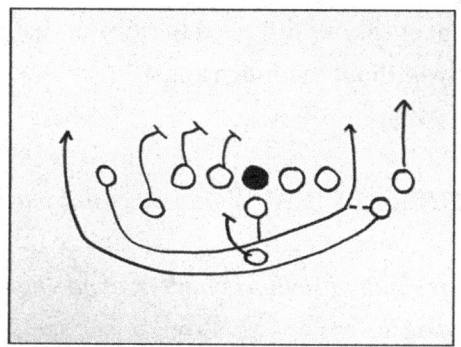

USING SPORTS METAPHORS AND ANALOGIES TO ILLUSTRATE AN IMPORTANT POINT

You've heard them before:
- Keep your eye on the ball.
- There's no "I" in team.
- Three strikes, you're out.
- Play to your strengths.
- Be in the moment.
- Keep it in the locker room.
- Act like you've been there before.
- Don't hurt the team.
- Stay home (translation: do your job).

Who doesn't love a great sports metaphor? How often have you been in a discussion and someone uses a sports term to explain a situation? The light bulb goes on. "Yeah, I understand what you're saying."

Sometimes a well-known sports phrase can be the easiest way to make a point. After all, *everyone* understands the basic goal of sports is to win. As Al Davis, the longtime owner of the Oakland Raiders football team, was known for saying, "Just win, baby." It can't get any more basic than that.

Sports references usually apply to behavior that contributes to success. It's pretty easy to understand, as a hitter in baseball, you better keep your eye on that incoming pitch in order to square it up. An outfielder who takes his eye off the flight of the ball will likely drop it.

As a Little Leaguer, you are coached, while at the plate, to watch the bat make contact with the ball and then to swing all the way through it. That will help you to get a hit.

It has often been said that the hardest thing to do in sports is to hit a baseball. You are asked to swing a round bat at a round ball and to hit it squarely.

You better keep your eye on the ball.

As a golfer, as you stand at the tee, you know you better watch the club strike the ball, or you will get embarrassing results.

Winning in sports is hard enough without introducing factors that may contribute to a mistake, or a loss. It's easy to visualize an athlete making a mistake. As sports fans, we've witnessed those situations. They make lasting impressions.

If a football team's right outside linebacker sees a sweep to the other side of the field and follows it too aggressively, he's going to be burned if it turns out to be a reverse. Thus, the concept of "staying home." Don't forget what your assignment is.

Sometimes, a coach will describe this as "trying to do too much." "Don't reach outside of your 'comfort zone,'" they will say. You don't need to take on someone else's assignment.

We once had a field technician in my department at Disney who got offtrack in doing his assignments. His real job was to do electrical/grip work. His position assisted the lighting director (or gaffer) in the setup of production lighting, power runs, lighting stands, flags, and scrims, etc. He was actually pretty skilled at it, and often was designated as the team lead or general lead.

But, for some reason, perhaps this idea of being the team boss gave him the notion he could do more. He began to arbitrarily drift to other things. He began asking talent if they had any needs he could help with. He ran errands for guests of the production. He offered to assist the producers. We once found him in the green room with talent, when he should have been on set with the crew.

By not "staying home" and doing his job, the other technicians on the production were now short-handed in accomplishing their assignments. Setup, take down, and company moves were impacted and taking longer, and running behind. Various production managers mentioned the problem to me. While we knew the individual, like the overeager linebacker, only wanted to help, he was hurting the team.

We had several discussions with the individual about focusing on his role. Interestingly, he thought he was providing unparalleled value—in his mind, a Disney difference—when taking on these tasks. Value that would bring more respect for himself and our team.

But that wasn't the case. When he continued to drift wayward on his assignments, we had to discipline him multiple times until, unfortunately, without an honest effort to correct this behavior, he finally had to be terminated.

Oh, how I wished he had realized the most basic of group tenets—there is no "I" in team!

AFTER FURTHER REVIEW: *What makes this play work?*

Okay, so this lesson isn't going to change the world. But sports are a great classroom of philosophy. And coaches are excellent teachers of that philosophy.

These philosophical lessons translate very well to the day-to-day situations we routinely encounter in life.

What makes sports metaphors so easy to understand is that they can be visualized. Anyone who's ever played baseball, or even played catch, knows what happens if you take your eye off the ball.

If you tell someone their effort is not up to par, or they're working on their third strike, they know exactly what that means.

The sports lessons we witness, and learn, are simple, though powerful messages for us. Good communication is always a staple of successful teams. And, sometimes, a valuable tool in that process can be the timely use of a well-known sports analogy or metaphor.

It just may produce that home run.

PLAY #14

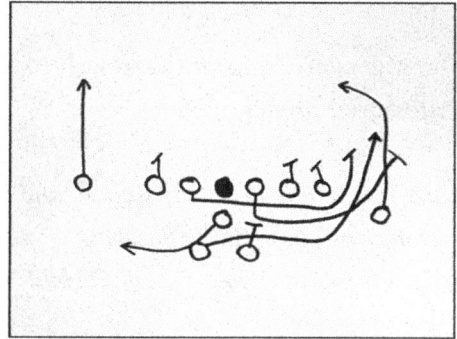

RESPECT THE TEAM'S
SOCIAL STRUCTURE

While Americans have a tremendous love of freedom, and will ardently remind anyone of its constitutional guarantee whenever they see a threat to it, powerful individuals like athletes realize there are necessary constraints in life.

One of those constraints is that when they are playing the game, the player recognizes the coach is in charge. The second is to not show up their teammates.

In most businesses, money talks. Those with the money usually have the most control and can dictate what they want. Though we have, as a nation, always encouraged individuals to speak up and to participate, to be involved, to demonstrate their individuality.

Generally, as a culture, Americans revere those who stand out. And in a lot of cases, that can be valuable to the cause.

But, sometimes, individuality can be a detriment in a business environment. If an individual is determined to openly question the efforts of the team leader, or another team member, that can adversely affect the cohesiveness and efficiency of the team and create a difficult environment for all involved.

But in sports, things are a little different. Those rich athletes—even the best-known superstars—know they need to listen to the coach. And they understand the importance of team camaraderie. A well-known sports axiom is to "keep it in the locker room." No one outside the team needs to know about disagreements between members of the team itself. Nothing good will come from that.

You need to show respect for each other for the sake of the team. For the sake of team unity.

The coach will decide who plays and how much time each player will get in the game. The coach will decide what offense will be run and what play will be called. The coach will call timeouts, make substitutions, and generally do his or her best to guide the team to success.

A superstar pitcher knows if the manager walks out to the mound and reaches out his hand for the baseball, you give it to him. You are being relieved. So please leave the field in a respectful fashion. And never do anything to show up the coach during the process.

And if the coach, or the manager, is doing a bad job and the team isn't winning, that will be dealt with by others. By those in position to make those decisions. So, as a player, just be professional and focus on doing *your* job.

Sports organizations are renowned for following the process and procedures. You show respect for your teammates and your coach or manager.

A player who can't get along with the coach, or management (such as football star Antonio Brown in 2019), will create a chasm that is going to distract from the team's overall goal and team camaraderie.

Sports teams will not allow that. Three teams—the Pittsburgh Steelers, the Oakland Raiders, and the New England Patriots—each had and then released Brown in 2019 because of various behavior-related issues.

Of course, circumstances may not be that transparent for a nonsports organization. HR departments are set up to listen to employee complaints. And if more execs in Hollywood had listened to complaints about sexual harassment, the violations that became the "Me Too" movement might have been avoided.

But, nevertheless, it can become too convenient for some in a corporate environment to voice their opinions about a matter, even when a little more sports-type discretion may be a better path.

Some companies may actually undermine their line-level leadership by empowering, and encouraging, their employees to voice their opinions about any subject bothering them.

Can you imagine what this would do to a sports team's chemistry if a player had carte blanche to go to the general manager or team president with any complaint he had regarding the coach or manager or a teammate? The discord and bad feelings generated would be devastating to the team's chances for success.

Just like a sports team, the untimely and disruptive actions of a business-world team member can also be damaging.

I have a theory that those with an understanding of sports principles would process these potentially explosive situations differently than someone unfamiliar with sports. To such an extent, the sports folks would likely not engage in those cases.

I say this because athletes, and those involved in sports, have learned throughout their lives that their actions may have some unintended ramifications. So, they are respectful of what they say and do.

From the time they were kids, athletes have heard about their bad in-game decision-making, the personal fouls they commit, the lack of concentration that allows an opponent to beat them one-on-one, the ill-advised remarks they make to others. And they have been admonished or chastised accordingly by their parents, friends, coaches, teammates, etc. for the impact their decisions had on the game or the team.

Now, cynics may say there is a difference between the sports-world social structure and the real-world social structure that doesn't cross over for this lesson. As in, sports teams have a unique sense of unity.

To that argument, because, as humans, we are always competing with each other for status, there may come a situation where the business-world individual may care more about himself than about the team and that sense of unity. The individual may become more concerned about his own survival. That's logical.

However, it is also known that respective cultures exist because the individuals that belong to them have similar personalities. That, too, creates a unique sense of unity.

For sure, the personalities attracted to the Disney organization I was so familiar with were certainly personalities that respected the ideals of the Disney culture and wanted to become part of it for that reason.

The Disney social structure didn't happen by accident. It was carefully crafted by founder Walt Disney and then handed over to the seasoned executives who protected and built upon the values that Walt himself created.

Likewise, for the protection of any nonsports organization's own sense of purpose and mission, it makes sense that a little more consideration for the impact of one's individual actions would be in order.

Moreover, a nonsports organization's personalities can be more fragile than those on a sports team. A company's office environment sits on a much more delicate balance than a football team's.

A nonsports company's team member may be taken aback by another's selfish comments, or perceive them as a personal attack. Especially if the comments seem personally driven, undeserved, or come from someone seen as a difficult personality.

Jen Howk, Ph.D., a social scientist educated at Harvard University, who collaborates on the *Beat Your Genes* podcast with Dr. Doug Lisle, was discussing the results of the 2020 presidential election when she had an interesting observation about how other individuals (and circumstances) can generally impact us.

In the world at large, she explains, people always think what is occurring to them is worse than the reality.

"We live in a very small slice of time in reality and are prone to exaggerating our circumstances," she says. "We can't look backward or forward accurately (for perspective)."

Therefore, the present always resonates the loudest.

Given this propensity for misperception—and the possible impact our actions can have on the smooth operation of the company, organization, or team—may be reason enough for us to preach the enviable practice of erring on the side of understanding.

In that regard, showing a little sports-world respect within your group's social structure might be a good on-going process, as well. How could it hurt?

AFTER FURTHER REVIEW: *What makes this play work?*

We all have a place in our team's, or company's, social structure.

Athletes realize, despite the power of their influence, that team success requires an individual's respect for the infrastructure.

During a game, respect the position of the coach, and never undermine team unity by showing up a teammate in public.

Nonsports businesses have their own social structures as well, which can be affected negatively with careless, disrespectful behavior.

Be considerate of the environment you are in. It might be wise to think of the impact to the team before choosing a course of action that might be seen as criticism of a particular member or members of the group, or an attack of the team's purpose.

Just like the sports team, you are all in it together.

PLAY #15

FIND YOUR MOTIVATION

Athletes are uniquely able to find ways to become motivated:

- By the desire to validate their abilities to those who matter.
- By the desire to live out a childhood dream.
- By the desire to win a championship.
- By the desire to prove oneself after an injury.
- By the desire to refute the naysayers.

By the desire to do something extraordinary, as in the aspiration to give back to a grieving city, such as those illustrating the "Boston Strong" slogan after the Boston Marathon bombing in 2013 that killed three people and injured more than 200.

In paying tribute to "Boston Strong" that season, the Boston Red Sox won the World Series, after which two of its players placed the trophy at the Marathon finish line while hundreds of others sang "God Bless America."

Motivation is one of the few contributors to performance over which the individual has control.

Psychology teaches us that there are two principal influences in motivation:

- Outside forces, such as other people or events (called extrinsic);
- Inside forces, which come from within (called intrinsic).

Humans are motivated to better themselves and progress toward their full potential (self-actualization) by satisfying several levels of need, including food, safety, love, belonging, self-esteem.

Of course, a big deterrent may come from feeling a *lack* of motivation, which may be caused by a belief that a task is too big or too difficult or too inconceivable to achieve. Lack of motivation can also be caused by burnout or a lack of confidence or by a tendency for procrastination.

Thinking like an athlete, I have always found discipline to be an ally of motivation. An athlete needs to be very disciplined to reach a goal. It can't be a part-time endeavor.

That speaks to me. And, sports aside, I try to follow that thinking in the everyday living I do.

If I am pursuing a goal where the prevailing theory is that A + B = C, and C is the result I want, then that's the formula I will utilize. As a pragmatic thinker, I realize that constant discipline and commitment, while difficult and perhaps overwhelming for certain personalities, are part of what it takes to achieve anything.

For me, once I make up my mind, I am fully committed to that decision. Whether that winds up being a good or bad decision, we'll determine later and, if necessary, make an adjustment. As an example, I decided that 2020 was going to be my year to get healthy, though I didn't start out with a clear plan of how to get there.

A good friend of mine talked to me about going to the Dr. McDougall Health & Medical Center in Santa Rosa, California, to learn about changing my diet for the better. Growing up, our family used to eat red meat all the time, sometimes three times a day. And if it wasn't red meat, it was pork or chicken or cheese. I loved my mom's cheese enchiladas!

I knew our diet wasn't healthy, but I really enjoyed the food and saw no reason to worry about it. That is, until both my folks died at seventy-eight years of age—seven years apart—yet I noticed after the fact that several of their siblings lived longer, including into their 90s.

I began to recognize the correlation between food and longevity.

John McDougall, M.D., has been a proponent of whole-food, plant-based eating for over forty-five years. Dr. McDougall has written numerous books about the subject and is an expert on reversing the negative effects of our lifelong habit of eating high-fat, overly processed, calorically dense food.

Essentially, the normal American diet is about 30% fat and contributes to many of the health problems that make us sick and eventually kill us.

When I attended the three-day Intensive McDougall Program in March 2020, I had a number of nagging issues I attributed to age, even though, in comparison to others, I thought I was in excellent physical condition. People always tell me I look ten years younger than I am.

By March of 2020, I had taken statins for high cholesterol for about twenty-five years. I used to joke about the statins being my license to eat badly, though I was concerned about being on any drug for that period of time.

I was sure that someday someone would say to me, "Al, because you didn't get off that drug ten years ago, you are now going to die because of it!"

By March of 2020, I was also into my fifteenth year of taking a prescription known as omeprazole—a proton pump inhibitor—for my stomach issues caused by GERD (gastroesophageal reflux disease).

During the Intensive Weekend, I heard about how statins can cause chronic muscle pain and muscle atrophy. Coincidentally, my legs were hurting all the time at that point, particularly my quadriceps muscles, and if I had to get down on my knees for some gardening or whatever, I literally had to push myself off the ground to get to my feet again.

Why is this happening? I thought. *Is this the way it's going to be from now on?*

During another lecture that weekend, I heard that long-term use of proton pump inhibitors can cause osteoporosis—weakening of the bones. And the cited data was frightening.

Fifty-four million people are affected by osteoporosis. Over two million "fragility" fractures occur each year. Fifty percent of women, and 25% of men over fifty will suffer a fracture.

Hip fractures can be especially devastating. There is a 24% one-year mortality rate for patients over fifty with hip fractures. Only 15% of hip fracture patients are able to walk across a room after a year, and 25% of those with hip fractures end up in a nursing home.

That weekend I found my motivation: change the way I eat and get off the medications.

As any athlete knows, commitment is not accidental. You need to exercise discipline to get there. To revisit the Vince Lombardi quote used earlier (in "Play 2: Demonstrate Accountability"):

"Winning is not a sometime thing; it's an all the time thing. You don't do things right once in a while. You do them right all the time. Winning is habit."

So, I began the habit.

The McDougall Program has a slogan: "It's the food." I see that two ways: It's the food that is killing you. And it's the food that will save you.

I bought into the McDougall dietary restrictions: no animal fats (no beef, pork, chicken, or fish), no dairy (milk, cheese, butter, eggs, ice cream, etc.), and no oil of any kind.

Focus on eating starches (potatoes, rice, wheat, corn, oats, bread, pasta), and eat lots of vegetables and fruits.

Jeff Novick, M.S., R.D.N., the dietitian and nutritionist at the McDougall Program, calls me a "freak of nature"—which I take as a compliment—because I was one of only a few people they had seen, who was able to hear the information once and then make the drastic dietary changes without any reservation, or any backsliding.

I attribute it to the kind of discipline an athlete uses to meet the greatest of challenges. You make a commitment and you go for it.

After three months, I was able to get off both drugs. My last total cholesterol reading while on statins was 181. After six months *off the drug*, and eating the whole-food, plant-based, minimally-processed diet, my cholesterol was 184. Essentially even. And it should continue to drop over time.

My stomach is feeling so much better as well. No GERD. No acid reflux. No bloating. No stomach cramps from eating heavy food that always made me feel like I had overeaten and made me terribly uncomfortable.

With my old way of eating, I used to tell others, "As I get older, I can't eat as much, because doing so makes me feel miserable and uncomfortable."

But in eating the McDougall-approved diet, I now consume a lot of food—really, as much as I want, without complaint. Because of the increase in natural fiber, I have lost twenty-five pounds without really trying. I started the program at 168 pounds, so I didn't have a lot to lose, but now I weigh less than when I graduated from college more than forty years ago. The fiber has also eliminated a nagging problem I had with hemorrhoids for more than ten years.

My BMI (body mass index) is now 21, when the medical index for a healthy person shows a range between 18 and 24.9.

Moreover, my leg pain has completely gone away. The problems with getting up or down are no more. My gums are pinker and healthier. There's no bleeding when flossing. And better breath is a benefit, too, as a bad diet smells.

One of my biggest previous concerns was a nodule I had under my right jaw. I first noticed it about ten years ago. The timing scared me because my mom died a year earlier of lymphoma and, after taking some scans, my doctor said the nodule was a lymph node.

While I thought it was big, as it measured from the tip of my thumb to the knuckle, the doctor said not to worry about it, as it was unremarkable. But I did worry about it and kept monitoring its size.

By the beginning of 2020, it hurt every day as it pressed on the nerves under my jaw. I found myself trying not to look down and to the right because that caused pain.

But now that I'm eating the right way for my body, the nodule is half the size it used to be and it doesn't hurt at all. Now it *really is* unremarkable.

It's our food choices that make us what we are—either sick or healthy.

The body works very hard to live, despite what we do to it. My motivation was to give my body a better chance to live a long time.

I'm sure you have a current motivation just as compelling to you.

AFTER FURTHER REVIEW: *What makes this play work?*

Motivation is one of the few contributors to performance over which the individual has control.

We can do great things with the proper motivation. Sometimes, our motivation may come from a childhood dream or, perhaps, from the need to redeem a social injustice or to help a community heal or to prove our self-worth or to be healthy.

We can find many sources of motivation. And they may have nothing to do with athletics, though the practices we find in athletics—discipline and commitment—can help you.

What might be your motivation?

PLAY #16

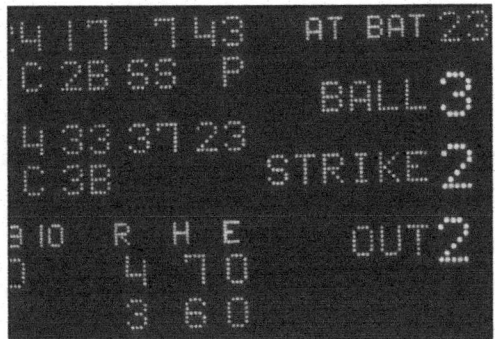

FINDING INSPIRATION IN
SPORTS' HEROIC MOMENTS

There are many settings where a gathered crowd might erupt in unison—during a popular song at a concert, at the conclusion of an enjoyable theatrical production, after an important political speech, but, perhaps, the most memorable are those dramatic achievements that occur during the most crucial moments of a tense sporting event.

Those moments are absolutely powerful. They can reflect the soul of a city. They become part of who we are.

In 1994 and 1995, the Houston Rockets won back-to-back NBA championships under the guidance of Coach Rudy Tomjanovich.

In playing their way from the sixth seed to the championship, the '95 Rockets were the lowest seed to ever become NBA champions, and on the floor after the clinching game, Tomjanovich proudly proclaimed, "Don't ever underestimate the heart of a champion."

How many other athletes, faced with their biggest challenges, have uttered that phrase since?

Athletes, at their best, at the most crucial moments, create those snapshots of which sports legends are made. The moments which define the impact of sports. The moments which forever rest in the long and glorious memories of sports fans. And the thunderous sound associated with those moments is the loudest sound imaginable.

I'll never forget where I was when Kirk Gibson hit that game-winning home run in the 1988 World Series.

I was in New York City for the wedding of a very close friend of mine, Loren Ledin, where I was to be his best man.

It was the opening game of the 1988 World Series between the Los Angeles Dodgers and Oakland Athletics—being played in Los Angeles—and I was in New York.

I took my girlfriend of that time, Diane, on that trip with me and convinced her to have dinner and watch the game from Mickey Mantle's bar across from Central Park. And, my god, Mickey Mantle was sitting there at the bar, standing out like the icon he was!

That would have been a good enough memory in itself.

Gibson was hurt and wasn't playing, and it didn't look like the Dodgers had any chance of beating a dominant and deep Oakland lineup featuring such stars as Mark McGwire and Jose Canseco, plus a stellar supporting group that included Dave Parker, Dave Henderson, and Carney Lansford. Oakland's star pitchers included Dave Stewart, the game one starter, and Dennis Eckersley, its exceptional closer.

The Dodgers scored first, with a two-run home run in the first inning. But then Canseco hit a grand slam in the second inning and I pretty much thought the game was over, spending much of the third through eighth innings periodically glancing over at Mickey Mantle.

Damn, that really is Mickey Mantle.

When the Dodgers came to bat in the ninth inning, down by a run (4–3) and facing Eckersley, I didn't expect much. There were two quick outs before pinch hitter Mike Davis worked a walk.

Then— surprise, surprise—Gibson, hobbling on two bad legs, was introduced as the pinch hitter. Vin Scully, the television game announcer and a baseball legend in his own right, exclaimed, "Look who's coming up!"

All of a sudden, there was a glimmer of hope. I perked up as the crowd noise swelled.

As Gibson reached home plate and took some practice swings, Scully, the Dodgers' longtime announcer, added, "All year long, they have looked to him to light the fire and, all year long, he answered the demands, until he was physically unable to start tonight with two bad legs." Scully's superb ability to frame up the story always made the game better.

Fans in attendance at Dodger Stadium would regularly listen to Scully on the radio because of the way he made the game better.

I remember looking over at Diane and saying with some incredulity, "They could actually win this game. A home run would win the game, and this is the one guy on the team capable of hitting that home run."

Scully continued, "And with two outs, you talk about the roll of the dice . . . this is it. If he hits the ball on the ground, I would imagine he would be running fifty percent. The Dodgers are trying to catch lightning, *right now.*"

The at bat started with two quick strikes—not looking good— before Gibson fouled off several pitches and took three balls to battle to a full count—three balls and two strikes.

The L.A. crowd was standing and screaming, hoping for a Hollywood movie ending. After Davis stole second base, and now with that 3–2 count, Gibson reapproached home plate for the climactic moment.

But like someone touching a live electrical wire, he abruptly backed away, calling time-out. He backpedaled for a few seconds to think about it, tapping his spikes with his bat a few times. Finally, he stepped back in and with the growing anticipation of the 55,000 people in attendance and a national television audience, Eckersley leaned in to hurl that one last pitch.

Timing it perfectly, Gibson used the strength of his arms to hit a line drive that became a historic home run.

Fittingly, the reaction of the crowd that was dialed up matched the moment—I could only imagine how much louder it sounded in Dodger Stadium.

Scully, understanding the magnitude of the achievement, made an astute storytelling decision by letting it play out for more than a minute without saying a word. The crowd's reaction was deafening. And the television images needed no narration.

Finally, Scully summed it up perfectly by saying, "In a season that has been so improbable, the *impossible* has happened."

It was as dramatic as a great movie. But real, and so much better. It was the kind of moment that permits us, as everyday people living ordinary lives, to continue to dream in our own lives because, sometimes, dreams do come true.

Sports allow us the fantasy to think we can be heroes, too. You, as a member of the sales team, can, at the eleventh hour, put in the effort to pull back the deal that looked like it was going to your competitor.

Sports achievement during the most difficult of circumstances permits us to believe anything can happen. Sports give us the permission to think big, to play big, to not be afraid of challenging situations.

Put us in, coach, and let us take that swing.

AFTER FURTHER REVIEW: *What makes this play work?*

We get tremendous inspiration from the great moments in sports. These are the moments which inspire lifetime memories and give us justification to believe the impossible can happen.

And if we have been fortunate enough to experience such a moment ourselves, we are more than happy to share that story with others who weren't there, to explain how a moment like that makes you feel.

There's nothing like incredible memories to push us when we think we can't go any farther.

To give us a reason to continue on.

To give us hope when hope is running out.

PLAY #17

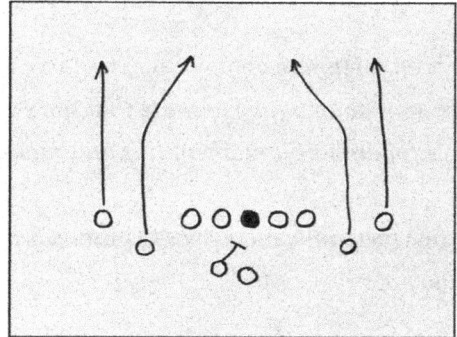

MAKING THE PROPER ADJUSTMENTS

Each week, a team's coaching staff will study an upcoming opponent by watching tape of that team's previous games, in order to understand what they will be facing.

What are that team's strengths? What are their weaknesses? Who are their best players, and what kinds of skills do those players possess? What types of plays does that team run well? What types of plays are less successful for them?

In football, you want to know if your opponent is a running team or a passing team, or good at both? How aggressive are they? What are their tendencies on third down? And what do they like to do in the red zone? Can their quarterback be rattled by a blitz? Or by shifting around your defensive players to disguise your line play or coverages? Which defensive schemes do they utilize, and what has been effective against them?

In baseball, you want to know how each batter on the opposing team handles the kind of pitches your pitchers will throw. What are their hot hitting zones versus their cold hitting zones? How should those hitters be played defensively? Who is experiencing a hitting streak, and who's in a slump? What kind of arms do the outfielders show? What kind of bullpen do they have?

In basketball, you will note if a team is big and gets most of their points in the paint, or is one that lives on the outside shot. How are they with the fast break? Who are their best defenders, shooters, passers, and rebounders? Who on their bench will cause us trouble?

Indeed, in all sports, it always comes down to what advantages can be exploited by your team, and how to minimize or correct your team's disadvantages.

It's planning and strategy.

Teams will put together a well-thought-out game plan that they feel gives themselves the best chance to win. But, despite spending a lot of time devising this game plan, there may still be problems.

If your basketball team is usually efficient with the three-point shots, but those shots aren't falling and you're getting beaten on the boards and the other team is streaking down the court for transition points, you better make some adjustments before things get too far out of hand.

Those adjustments may include bringing in the guy from your bench who provides "instant offense." Or a better rebounder. Or an energy guy who is adept in getting teammates engaged in the game. Or, perhaps, bringing in the whole second team. As they call it in hockey, a "line change."

The best coaches are usually adept at reading their teams to determine what tactic might stem the tide. What is needed right now? You build a deep bench of players with different skill sets exactly for these scenarios.

Sometimes, however, the other team is just better than yours and simple adjustments will not make enough of a difference to win the game.

It's critical for coaches, and team administrators, to recognize and admit their team's flaws and weaknesses. Only with honest evaluation can they then move to address the issues.

But it's also important to weigh the gravity of the circumstances. As a *Daily Trojan* copy editor in journalism school at USC, I remember this admonishment: Don't make a change (or edit) simply for the sake of making a change. If the copy works, leave it alone.

Phil Jackson, the basketball legend, didn't coach his teams to eleven NBA titles by scuttling the triangle offense for something more contemporary.

In college football, Nick Saban didn't win his seventh national championship (in January 2021) by abandoning his tried-and-true methods.

But good coaches like Saban have a feel for when a calculated adjustment is necessary, such as the one he made during the 2018 national championship game. Saban's #4 seeded Alabama Crimson Tide squad was playing Kirby Smart's #3 seeded Georgia Bulldogs team in that contest.

Alabama's offense featured the uber-successful Jalen Hurts as starting quarterback, a dual-threat sophomore who had compiled a 25–2 record as a two-year starter entering that game. Hurts appeared to be entrenched in his role. But he didn't play a very good first half, and Alabama was being outworked and on the losing end of a 13–0 score at halftime.

Earlier in this book, we described sports as a civilized version of war, and some concepts do cross over. An important Marine Corps axiom is to "improvise, adapt, and overcome" all obstacles in all situations. That is, to show the willingness and determination to keep fighting until victory is attained. In a similar way, Saban assessed what he needed to do to turn the game around.

Hurts' backup, Tua Tagovailoa, had played a mere "mop-up" role during the course of the season, only getting on the field when the game was in hand. But in a surprising move, Saban decided to put Tua in to play the entire second half.

As the coach explained after the game, "I thought Tua would give us a better chance and a spark, which he certainly did."

Tua, a true freshman and five-star recruit from Hawaii, threw three touchdowns in the second half and won the game with one of the more implausible plays in Alabama's storied history.

The game went to overtime with each team tied at twenty. Georgia had the ball first and took the lead with a long field goal of fifty-one yards to go up 23–20.

On the first play of Alabama's next possession, Tua was chased and sacked for a sixteen-yard loss, a huge mistake at that point of the game and one that seemingly gave all the momentum to Georgia.

The ball was now on the forty-one-yard line and Alabama needed to get to the fifteen-yard line for a first down.

On that second-and-26 play, Alabama sent all four of their receivers streaking downfield, and after looking off a safety like an experienced veteran . . . boom! Tua noticed a wide open DeVonta Smith racing down the left sideline.

Tua hit the speedy wideout in full stride and, with that bolt of lightning, the game was over and Alabama was the national champion.

Interestingly, Smith was also an unknown true freshman at the time, though he too went on to make a name for himself at Alabama as the 2020 Heisman Trophy winner. Nice to have so much available talent, huh?

I found my own need to make an important adjustment at Disneyland when we were first starting Broadcast Services (now known as Broadcast Production).

As I mentioned in "Play #5," we made a successful proposal to Disney's upper management to fund this unique area to generate video product and tactics, which the resort could use to market in a different way by proactively distributing broadcast product of our own and working directly with broadcast news organizations to assist with their coverage of the resort during its thirtieth anniversary year.

This was kind of like discovering the Crock-pot. Wow, what great things can we now make that will simmer in their own scrumptiousness while we are doing other stuff?

While we started by producing video news releases of car winners, and then EPKs (electronic press kits), I enjoyed pushing the envelope to find new things for the area to take on. It was now 1986, a year after our formation. What more could we do?

Because we had obtained the capital to install transmission equipment to send microwave signals like a TV news van to a relay point at nearby Santiago Peak, which could then be transmitted by a variety of means to stations around the country, we decided to technically offer "live" news shots and "live" TV programming opportunities for TV stations interested in broadcasting from the Disneyland Resort.

Live remote coverage was acquiring great cachet with the broadcast media, and the chance to produce these remotes from within the boundaries of the Disneyland Resort was a new and cool idea. And we found that stations were very open to broadcasting from "The Happiest Place on Earth." They thought it would be of interest to their viewers.

So, there we were, breaking new ground by working with a network affiliate from San Diego, which agreed to be the first to broadcast their entire mid-day news show from the Disneyland Resort.

In 1986, we were still giving away new cars, and the 3D short movie, *Captain EO*, featuring Michael Jackson, was about to open in Tomorrowland. I was excited by this new broadcast venture. It would be a wonderful next step for the department.

We borrowed some technicians from the Entertainment Division's Tech Services department and added some Orange County freelancers to fill out camera, audio, and lighting positions for the crew—but the crew was not versed in live television production. And we unwittingly didn't schedule enough crew members. Those deficits showed quickly enough.

A few minutes into the show, which we were broadcasting from the Space Mountain concourse level, one of the lights on the set went dark, putting half of the set and one of the news anchors, in shadow. The power required for the HMI television lighting had tripped a breaker.

The audio guy from Tech Services was familiar with the location and said, "I know where the power panel is; I'll take care of it," and he ran off.

While he was gone, and the set was still in darkness, the main anchor's microphone stopped working. But because the audio guy—the only audio guy—was off doing the electric work, there was no one to address the microphone issue. The two anchors were forced to awkwardly pass a microphone back and forth for their respective pieces.

So much for Disney excellence. It may have been the longest hour of my career. The show was a disaster and our friends from San Diego left very upset.

This led to a detailed postmortem to evaluate our mistakes and our miscalculations and work through a comprehensive new plan for doing live broadcasts. We realized that, like a struggling sports team, we had significant disadvantages in trying to accomplish something we were not built for—e.g., doing live broadcasts from a working theme park.

As I often explained to new executives and new team members until I retired, doing live broadcast is a very fragile business and, to earn the trust of industry broadcasters, we would have to *exceed* their expectations.

We had to overcome the bias that a theme park group could actually accomplish a live broadcast. There was the running joke, "Where do you work when you're not doing broadcast—on the Jungle Cruise?"

So, after careful consideration, we made the following adjustments:

(1) Where we didn't have the right talent at Disneyland to execute TV production, it was imperative that we hire, as freelancers, experienced and recommended broadcast professionals from Los Angeles/Hollywood. While I was still at the resort, we put as many as 400 of these individuals on professional services contracts for key roles such as camera operators, lighting directors, grip/electrics, audio technicians and audio integrators, engineers, editors, stylists, and makeup artists.

(2) Bring in our own power generators for live production or use on-site power specifically installed and earmarked for our broadcast needs. While the cost of such permanent installations—as capital improvements—called for executive-level approval, this investment provided a Disney difference, as it eliminated the sharing of house facilities with other operating areas such as attractions, stores, or restaurants, where that sharing could threaten their functional efficiency, as well as our production success.

(3) Schedule rehearsal and/or testing days in advance of live production days, particularly for major events.

(4) Call on key industry broadcast consultants to assist the broadcast team, as needed, when planning high-profile and/ or especially difficult projects, such as the major media openings for Disney California Adventure, Downtown Disney, significant resort anniversaries, and every major attraction and land opening after 1985.

This included the 2019 opening of *"Star Wars*: Galaxy's Edge," where Broadcast Production technically planned and completed three days of taped segments and live broadcasts for stations throughout the country.

For major events like Galaxy's Edge, the Broadcast Production team would actually expand to a group of 400 people in order to properly implement all the broadcast elements.

During that event, we didn't just successfully execute one live signal, or two, but eleven separate live signals sent simultaneously from eleven different "stand-up" locations within the land. In addition, we managed two additional locations for various network hits, two for various local Los Angeles stations using their own equipment, one for *Entertainment Tonight* to tape that day's show, and a wireless roving crew executing live hits for *Good Morning America*.

Organizing a broadcast schedule of that scale is something that a visiting producer from ESPN told me the networks would find daunting.

Thankfully, over the years, our learned and refined processes returned the success we wanted and rewarded us with a reputation among broadcast professionals—those at TV networks and TV stations—for doing it right.

Undoubtedly, every team is going to have adversity. Both as individuals, and as a unit, we are only as good as we are at any one moment.

During the 2020 American Football Conference Championship game, Mecole Hardman, a Kansas City Chiefs wide receiver and return specialist, muffed a first quarter punt inside the Chiefs' five-yard line.

The Buffalo Bills recovered the ball and used that gift to take a 9–0 lead into the second quarter. But Hardman redeemed himself with a much better moment—a spectacular fifty-yard end around, setting a Chiefs franchise record for the longest run from scrimmage in a playoff game.

Then Hardman followed that with a three-yard touchdown reception from quarterback Patrick Mahomes, after which star tight end Travis Kelce congratulated Hardman by saying, "That's how you handle adversity. You smack it right in the mouth!"

AFTER FURTHER REVIEW: *What makes this play work?*

Adversity is an unfortunate part of the human experience.

While sports teams will spend a lot of time and effort to produce a perfect game plan, it is very unlikely the game will be played out flawlessly.

It is just as probable that we will see in life, as much as we do in sports, a need to make midstream adjustments to overcome difficult circumstances.

Occasionally, we need to seriously evaluate our personal and team issues as well as significant mistakes and, sometimes, deep-rooted miscalculations in order to devise a more efficient operation.

By being honest with ourselves and looking at our strengths and weaknesses strategically, and objectively, we can arrive at the proper adjustments—whether they be minute modifications, moderate substitutions, or wholesale changes.

PLAY #18

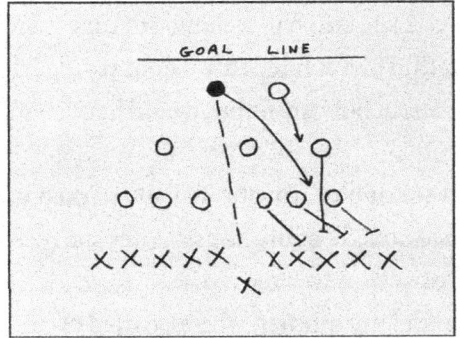

DON'T GIVE UP, THINGS CAN TURN AROUND

Life isn't fair. Despite the faith we put in our God, despite the honest lives we may lead, despite the respectful way we may treat others, each of us has been or will be presented with unfair circumstances to surmount.

You have a family member who has been diagnosed with cancer. It's shocking and heartbreaking and many people who find themselves in this undeserved situation become depressed.

Years ago, while my father was battling stage 4 stomach cancer, I had a neighbor who was diagnosed with stage 2 breast cancer. What resonated with me at the time was how easily she gave up.

Her doctor had set up a series of appointments for treatment, and her brother, whom she lived with, had arranged special transportation to the appointments and back.

She didn't go to any of them. She essentially accepted her time was going to end, and in three short months of doing nothing to fight for her life, it was over.

When she told me what she was going to do, I retreated to my high conscientious personality trait to try to talk her out of it. After all, I said, at stage 2 she still had a chance to turn it around. "If you're going to go out, don't let it happen without trying," I urged.

I thought about how my father would have changed places with her in an instant.

She had a small blue Toyota that she parked under a tree in a community space outside of my house. After she received her cancer diagnosis, that car was never moved.

My father and my mother, who also died of cancer (my mother had lymphoma), both lived for seven years after being diagnosed with stage 4 cancer. I attribute that stubbornness to their respective tenacity for life, and their refusal to give up because of their devotion to our family.

Those of us who love sports are inspired that sometimes, when things are going badly and the cause looks lost, the game will turn around. It does happen.

There's a long list of those occasions. And the more remarkable ones live long in our memories. So, don't give up.

As a student, and editor of the USC *Daily Trojan* student newspaper, I attended one of the most famous USC football games ever played. It was 1974 and USC was playing its intersectional rival Notre Dame in the Los Angeles Coliseum.

Notre Dame was whipping SC in the first half, 24–0, and things were looking bleak when, just before halftime, the Trojans worked their way down the field for a touchdown to close the deficit to 24–6.

Both teams were really good, and a game against Notre Dame always carries extra amperage to it, so what happened in the second half is stuff of college football legend.

At halftime, USC coach John McKay told the team it needed to score the first time it had the ball in the second half. He expected Notre Dame to kick off to SC's outstanding tailback, Anthony Davis, and in an example of his exceptional wit, McKay reminded his team it was not against NCAA rules to block on kickoffs.

As the story goes, one of McKay's assistant coaches then challenged the special teams' players one by one with the exhortation: "YOU block somebody! And YOU block somebody! And YOU block somebody!"

Davis, a Notre Dame nemesis, who scored six touchdowns against them in the 1972 game, caught the kickoff two yards into the end zone, and following some exceptional blocking, shook the Coliseum into a frenzy when he returned the ball 102 yards for a touchdown.

SC scored forty-nine unanswered points in the second half—thirty-five points in the third quarter alone—as they rumbled to a stunning 55–24 victory.

USC's defense was as dominant as their offense, grabbing three interceptions and forcing two fumbles in the second half to contribute to the spectacular turnaround.

Such incredible reversals of fortune give us regular folks reason to believe if we just make the best of bad situations, good things may happen.

As described in the previous chapter, in-game situations in sports often call for making adjustments. And the best coaches and best players are really good at it.

How often have you heard the phrase, "They're a second-half team."? That usually refers to a team that is skilled at reviewing what its opponent did in the first half and then successfully makes the adjustments to counter it.

There's a saying in sports to "take what they're giving you," because your opponent usually can't take away everything.

Teams good at adapting will put in the effort to force things to turn around. It's a matter of effort. And if the circumstances improve, the team doesn't relax at that point.

Then it's about capturing the momentum. Those elements: making adjustments, utilizing the best options available, and then seizing the momentum and pushing to victory can happen in everyday life, too.

Why not believe if we control our own attitude when things are going awry and put in some extra effort, our effort may be rewarded? Call it the assistance of God, or fate, or just good luck. Whatever it is, it's possible for other things in life to imitate the miraculous endings we see in sports.

For those of us who integrate sports philosophies so much into our regular lives, we almost expect it.

AFTER FURTHER REVIEW: *What makes this play work?*

Perhaps nowhere do we see the impact of momentum more than in sports.

As dire as things may look at the moment, a change of fortune can turn things around. As the quote from New York Yankees great Yogi Berra goes, "It ain't over till it's over."

What Yogi likely meant by that quote was that unexpected things do occur and can affect the outcome. So, we should always stay vigilant and focused on the task, and most important, not give up.

A positive frame of mind can be an unstoppable force.

PLAY #19

BELIEVE IN YOURSELF /
BELIEVE IN YOUR SKILLS

Confidence, or lack of it, can be debilitating.

It's amazing how easy it is for athletes to lose their confidence, which is an interesting phenomenon when considering how skilled professional athletes are.

There are only about 750 total players on MLB rosters. Only about 450 total players on NBA rosters. And while there are 1,696 active players on NFL rosters, relative to the population of the United States (just shy of 332 million people as of 2020), that means only .0005% of the population can play in the NFL. So, you've got to be incredibly good to play a professional sport.

Still, these athletes can be hampered by a lack of confidence. And we see it occur all the time:

- A basketball player who has a stretch where he can't make a shot.
- A golfer with putting problems.
- A running back with fumbling problems.
- A tennis player who can't get his first serve in.

In 1983, the Los Angeles Dodgers had an infielder, Steve Sax, who had problems making the routine throw from his second base position to first base.

That same year, Dodgers' third baseman Pedro Guerrero, who had his own confidence problems, was asked what he thought about in a close game. His remark: "I'm only thinking about two things. First, I hope they don't hit the ball to me. Number two, I hope they don't hit it to Sax."

The award for the "least confident" athlete, however, has to go to any baseball player in a slump. Part of that is the general difficulty of a sport where the superstars only succeed 30% of the time (the .300 hitters). As baseball players will say, the game is humbling.

Despite years of refining their craft, honing their skills, and studying pitchers, a slump can cause a hitter to severely doubt himself. And without confidence, that hitter will be overmatched against a quality Major League pitcher.

Hitters in a slump will tinker with their swings and their stance, how they step into a pitch, the bat they use, the rituals they practice, even what they eat, or what they wear.

Athletes can be amazingly superstitious. To feel confident, sometimes they will repeat their rituals over and over again, in the same way.

Nomar Garciaparra, an infielder who played for the Boston Red Sox, Chicago Cubs, Los Angeles Dodgers, and the Oakland Athletics, had a habit of adjusting the wristbands on his batting gloves and tapping the toes of both feet as he stepped into the batter's box. And many times, he would do it again between swings.

When I was in the Disneyland Resort Publicity department in the late '70s and early '80s, we had a relationship with L.A. Dodgers' star Steve Garvey, a ten-time all-star who won the National League Most Valuable Player Award in 1974 and had six 200-hit seasons during his career.

During one visit to the resort with his wife of the time, Cyndy, and their two daughters, Cyndy told me she could always tell when Steve was going to get a hit. "When he wiggles his butt a certain way as he's preparing to swing the bat, he gets a hit."

Apparently, Steve wiggled his butt 2,599 times during his nineteen-year career, as that was the number of hits he totaled.

The human spirit can be pushed off-track. But that same spirit can pull itself back together as well, especially with a convincing and well-timed hit of esteem.

Perhaps this is where the pep talk originated?

Just about every great speech from a coach has something to do with him believing in his team and declaring he would only want to go to "war" with them.

He will tell them if they just do what they do well, what they practice every single day, and what they have trained themselves to do all their lives, they will win!

Sometimes a coach will advise a player not to think too much. "Just trust your skills." This emphasizes what our friend Yogi Berra speculated in another of his famous quotes: "How can you think and hit at the same time?"

Yogi also offered this malaprop: "Baseball is 90% mental. The other half is physical."

While, again, these athletes probably have adequate physical skills, gaining confidence is a significant mental exercise. And it can be fragile.

There are organizations now which help athletes with the mental part of sports by teaching them how to stay positive and to prepare for the challenges that inevitably occur. Part of this is ignoring the negative energy that can develop during a game.

One of the philosophies that coaches preach to their quarterbacks is to "have a short-term memory." In other words, forget about that last pass that was intercepted, or that errant throw you made. Just focus on the next play.

Now, for sure, confidence plays into the success of business-world employees, as well.

Yogi Berra's description of baseball being 90% mental is probably a better description of work in the everyday business world, where your ability to think, and how you process the environment around you, is more important than physical skills.

Without a doubt, a little bit of a sports pep talk, or positive thinking, can help a lot of people who lack the confidence in business situations.

After all, if you are not experienced in pitching an idea to your boss, or your team, or a client, of course you will get nervous. And if you are unsure about your skills, you may be reluctant to put yourself in situations where others may judge you, if just to avoid the possible embarrassment.

My friend Mike Hyland, whom I mentioned earlier, is very adept at public relations strategy and pitching the plans he advocates, but he admits he can still get nervous when presenting to the top leaders of the Disney company.

He once told me an amusing story about getting so nervous about a particularly important presentation, his thumbs began to sweat.

He joked it was so bad he had to wrap a towel around each thumb to prevent a pool of water from gathering. A funny visual which actually didn't happen, but a great example of his self-deprecating sense of humor. It's also evidence that even the most experienced professionals can be subject to a lack of confidence.

If I had been there, perhaps I could have provided support with my own sports-type pep talk:

"Mike, you are really good at explaining these situations. Just focus on the task. Go through your progressions—your points—one by one. Relax, believe in your ideas, and go in there and *do* your thing!"

AFTER FURTHER REVIEW: *What makes this play work?*

Even great athletes lack confidence at times. This is not a sign of weakness.

Doing something wrong once reminds you it can happen again, and sometimes people fall into bad habits.

Thinking too much about things, while not an easy situation to avoid, usually just causes more angst.

Focus on positive thinking. What, specifically, can you do to be successful? Avoid the negativity. Follow your script. Trust your training.

If you are new or young or inexperienced and unproven, this is your chance to show you belong.

Believe in yourself and believe in your skills. You were given that job for a reason—others believe in you. Now go, prove them right!!!

PLAY #20

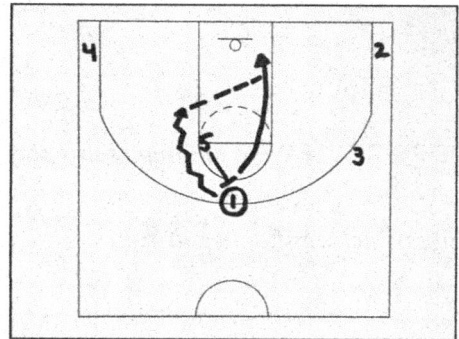

YOU CAN'T WIN THEM ALL, SO LEARN TO BE A GOOD SPORT

Even the best sports franchises will hit a rough patch.

Even talented teams can be beset by devastating injuries, bad luck, or lack of team chemistry.

Even the best coaches will make a bad decision that loses a game.

Even the best players will have a bad game, or an off year.

All of those scenarios will occur, and it's during times like those when the character nurtured by sports comes into play. And an athlete's public response to a loss can serve as a wonderful example for the rest of us to emulate in our own lives.

How many of us get angry when circumstances turn against us?

How many of us say vicious things to those we believe did us wrong?

We all want things to go our way.

For those of us with more disagreeable personalities, we may need good fortune to lean our way more often than others in order to be happy. An 80/20 trader needs to get things his or her way eighty percent of the time to be satisfied.

In sports, that may not be possible. This is where respect for the game, and for those who play it, comes into play.

Athletes are role models, and whether they like it or not, their place in public opinion will be measured by how they act, and the behavior they exhibit.

Athletes who show dignity after a tough loss are respected for reacting the right way. For sure, their fans are watching. And when a loss is accepted the right way, fans will appreciate that response and return it with higher praise when a win is achieved.

One of my favorite sports rituals is the handshake line created by the two teams playing for the Stanley Cup, the National Hockey League's championship trophy.

After the Cup has been won, every player from each team lines up on the ice and, one by one, they make the progression to congratulate each member of the opposite team for a hard-fought series. And as physical as ice hockey is, it's always a hard-fought series!

I appreciate this classy parade of respect.

I have also come to respect college football programs for having the insight to teach their athletes how to deal with the media. For the higher profile programs, and the higher profile players who may interact with the media regularly, it's impressive to see how, as teenagers, they are learning to display the lessons of sportsmanship.

These athletes learn the process of politely and articulately answering questions and demonstrating respect to others, even during difficult losses. You can see them getting better with more experience, as they get closer to becoming professional players, where the scrutiny is even greater.

My friend Loren Ledin, the Prep Editor for the Ventura County Star in Southern California, says that the larger high school programs are also engaging in the practice of making players available to the media to give them the opportunities to learn before they get to college.

We all want to feel good about our interactions with sports and those who participate in them. Because of the prominent nature of sports, our kids will look up to the athletes they admire. We want our heroes to be good people.

Of course, examples of sportsmanship, or how we treat others, should extend beyond the athletes themselves, to all of us.

No one likes a bad loser.

How many of us have seen video of an out-of-control parent who makes an ugly scene at his or her child's baseball game, football game, or soccer game?

Such embarrassing episodes remind us that, as adults, we should be the responsible ones displaying the proper way for a human to act under disappointing circumstances.

There's a great example from the movie *The Karate Kid*, where the sage and mentor, Mr. Miyagi, says, "Karate begins and ends with courtesy. This means respect others, refrain from violent behavior, practice fairness in the spirit of good sportsmanship."

There's no replacement for good character and integrity. That's why we admire and gravitate to those who have such qualities—whether in sports, in business, or in the community around us.

AFTER FURTHER REVIEW: *What makes this play work?*

Sooner or later, even the most successful of us are going to lose at something. While losing is hard, particularly for the most competitive, learning to lose gracefully is a respected art form. Those who do this well are likely to earn more respect for the example they exhibit.

It may be difficult in the workplace when someone has appeared to undermine your position or has rejected one of your ideas, but taking it in stride and using it as motivation to do better will be viewed with approval.

People who matter to you are watching how you act—your leaders, peers, and subordinates—and will return the proper respect if you act responsibly.

PLAY #21

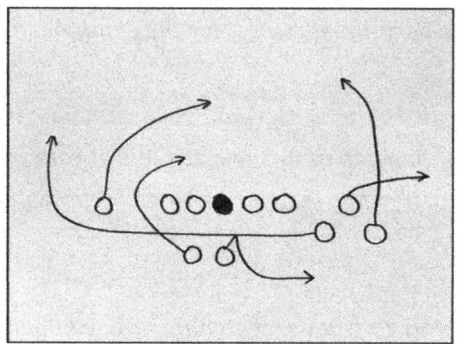

FINISH

At the end of the third quarter of a high school or college football game, you may see the players raise a hand in the air, showing four fingers. This is their reminder, as they walk to the other end of the field to begin the fourth quarter, to "finish strong." A reminder obviously drilled into the players' heads by their coaches.

While you may be tired or beaten up by the game's physicality, now is not the time to mentally let down.

You play the game the same way for four quarters or forty-eight minutes (if it's basketball) or for twenty-seven outs (if it's baseball). You play as hard—or harder—in the final two minutes of the game as you did in the first two minutes.

As a construction crew foreman, you wouldn't stop before the completion of a house. You're not done until that last stroke of paint or until that last item is checked off the list of changes.

If you're on a diet and want to lose twenty pounds, you are not done when you reach fifteen. Keep it going. Don't let up. Show the fortitude to finish it off.

During the 2020 college football season, then USC offensive line coach Tim Drevno explained during a media interview how he preached the concept of "strain to finish" to his players. Essentially, putting in whatever extra effort is needed to meet your objective.

I liken it to the effort a sprinter puts in at the end of a hundred-meter race. The sprinter doesn't coast across the finish line. Instead, that sprinter will lean hard into the finish, straining with all he or she has to break the imaginary tape.

By doing that, and by shaving hundreds of a second off the time, can be the difference between winning or not, or better yet, setting a record.

Drevno mentioned that during the final minutes of the 2020 USC–Arizona game, with the contest on the line, one of his linemen, Andrew Vorhees, missed a block in the red zone. But Vorhees continued to play, moving toward the goal line to assist the running back (Vavae Malepeai) to score the winning touchdown.

As Drevno said, "If you strain to finish, there's a good chance that something good is gonna happen."

In a lot of ways, mindset is again the key element here.

As we talked about in "Play #19" regarding confidence and believing in yourself and your skills, the wrong mental attitude can impact your performance, including how you finish.

How many times have you seen a team that loses more than their share of close games? During those situations, the players—especially the team's younger players—may say, "We need to learn how to win."

That's because there aren't any moral victories in competitive sports. It doesn't matter how many times you come close. It's not like the intramural school team that doesn't keep score for the sake of avoiding negative feelings. In the real world, you are usually judged by how you succeed. Or how you don't.

Maintaining a mental edge is important.

Say a football team plays well for three quarters. The players are aggressive, playing quickly and with confidence, making plays on offense, and running to the ball and hitting the opponent hard on defense. They have a positive mindset.

But things turn around in the fourth quarter and the team begins to look different and tentative. What causes that?

Perhaps they begin to worry about losing and begin to feel the pressure to win? Sometimes, they are playing *not* to lose.

But teams that go for the knockout blow in the fourth quarter are maintaining the same attitude throughout the game.

To finish strong, a player should ask himself: "What do I need to do to *dictate* the action on *this* play?"

The player can prepare for crucial moments by reminding himself to "be aggressive," "be smart," and "be ready."

Some players develop a reputation for being "finishers": Joe Montana, Russell Wilson, Michael Jordan, Kobe Bryant.

Kobe actually finished his career in a way that, philosophically, perfectly modeled the way he played his entire life.

On April 12, 2013, Kobe Bryant, at age thirty-four, tore an Achilles tendon in a game against the Golden State Warriors, perhaps the most difficult injury for an older athlete to come back from. Very few professional athletes can return from that injury to be close to what they were before.

But, Kobe, as we detailed earlier, was a freak even among athletes, and if anyone was going to do it, it was going to be Kobe.

As an example of his toughness, during his fall to the floor, a foul was called on Kobe's defender. After leaving the court briefly, Kobe literally shuffled to the free throw line to make his two shots and tie up the game, 109–109, that the Lakers would ultimately win.

In the locker room after the game, Kobe was expectedly tearful and distraught. He talked about the difficulty of accepting such an injury after all he had worked for as he pondered next steps.

When a reporter asked if he could possibly return from this injury like he had others, through plain willpower, Kobe said, "No, I can't even walk."

During the next year, Kobe spent a lot of time rehabbing as he reached out to others who had sustained the injury in order to understand their best practices.

Before the end of the 2013–14 season, he was able to return to play six games and average 13.8 points per game, shooting a respectable 42.5%.

The next year, the 2014–15 season, he played thirty-five games and averaged 22.3 points per game, though he shot a sub-par 37.3%.

Kobe decided to make the next year his final year, and he played in sixty-six of the eighty-two games, but averaged a relatively low (for him) 17.6 points per game and only shot 35.8% for the season. But he made it a priority to enjoy the final year of his career, as he received well-earned "good-bye" salutes at NBA arenas throughout the league.

In a spectacular final performance, at Los Angeles' Staples Center arena, Kobe did something truly special for all his fans. With hundreds of media witnessing the occasion, and fans excitedly chanting "Ko-be, Ko-be," he pushed his exhausted body to score sixty points in a come-from-behind Lakers victory. It was the most points any NBA player had ever scored in the final game of his career.

And after a post-game, on-court celebration in which he thanked all the fans for their many years of support, Kobe, feeling satisfied that he had left it all on the floor, concluded by tapping his chest and saying, "Mamba out," as he laid the microphone on the court.

A remarkable finish.

AFTER FURTHER REVIEW: *What makes this play work?*

Being tired is not an excuse for not finishing well. In sports, moral victories don't matter. You don't get kudos for simply being close. There's nothing special about that.

You need the mental and physical fortitude to finish the right way both in sports and in whatever critical tasks life may bring your way.

Much of that is mental. Maintaining the right frame of mind. And not allowing yourself to fall into negative thinking when things start to go bad. Or to bail out completely when the tasks become difficult.

Find the right mental practices for yourself—a reminder of what you can do to dictate a successful outcome; a reminder to be proactive and not take the easy way out.

A reminder to strain to finish.

THE POST-GAME SPEECH: MEETING LIFE'S CHALLENGES

My mom, rest her soul, was a big fan of the TV show *Dancing with the Stars*. During the last few years of her life, we used to plan a weekly phone call each Monday night and it would invariably coincide with that evening's episode of *DWTS*.

It began one night during the Donny Osmond season, when my mom said to me, "Oh, I have to go. *Dancing with the Stars* is on and I want to see Donny Osmond."

I responded, "Don't hang up. Let me turn it on as well. I'd like to see how he does too, and we can talk about it."

That became a Monday ritual for us.

Dancing with the Stars was a regular visitor to the Disneyland Resort, and I enjoyed working with that team and respected the quality with which they produced their show. Their production design and technical work were always impressive, and as a self-professed perfectionist, I admired the high standards of *DWTS*.

I mention this show for another reason. It is not a coincidence that so many athletes have won the respective seasons of the show. In the twenty-nine seasons of the show (as of November, 2020), eleven times the winner was an athlete. I remember having this conversation with my mom several times when noting that athletes are adept at pushing themselves through big challenges.

While individuals appearing on that TV show may not have an affinity to learn the samba or Argentine tango, or any of the other dances, nevertheless, an athlete would not be rebuffed by the tough criticism of the judges or ever consider just going through the motions to complete a difficult dancing assignment.

In the life of an athlete, the tougher the assignment, the greater the reward, and the harder they work.

You know the old line from *A League of Their Own* that there is "no crying in baseball"? Well, there is no quitting, either. Being emotionally and psychologically pushed by a coach or teammate is just a regular part of the job.

So, to me, *Dancing with the Stars* is a real example of the point of this book: using sports processes to help us succeed in other parts of life, like making a commitment to learn to dance well enough to win a TV show.

In a January 2021 *Los Angeles Times* article commemorating the first anniversary of Kobe Bryant's death, Dave Belasco, an adjunct professor at the USC Marshall School of Business, had this comment about Kobe's numerous post-retirement achievements:

"I was really inspired by someone who was known to be an elite athlete shifting gears and trying to do something that was very different and very bold. I think many of the skills and the mindset that he used to excel in sports served him perfectly in business."

Learning, and living, with such proven sports methods can become part of our persona. They can become part of how we deal with the world.

For myself, I have been thinking so long like a sports guy that it has become second nature—and instinct—to me. It's like ducking when something is coming at your head.

In 1983, I was a victim of a really bad auto accident where my car was rear-ended, while sitting at a red light, by a car that was estimated, by witnesses, to be traveling at sixty miles an hour.

While it was 3:00 p.m. on a lazy Sunday afternoon, the other driver had fallen asleep at the wheel. He was unharmed, but I sustained a broken neck at C2, the second cervical vertebra, otherwise known as the "hangman's fracture," as that is where the neck breaks during a hanging.

The car I was driving, a 280Z, was pushed through the intersection, up over a curb, and 150 feet into an open field where it stopped, scrunched so badly that the "jaws of life" had to be used to pry the doors open.

I spent four days in the intensive care unit and thirty days in the hospital before going home, and I was in a halo neck brace for three and a half months.

A halo brace is the device doctors use in these cases. It involves a circular bar which surrounds the head and is screwed into the skull at four points (think constant headache) and attaches to four vertical bars that connect to a vest. The idea is to isolate your neck so you can't move it while it is healing.

It can take anywhere from three months to a year for the neck to heal, depending on how fast the body works and any complications.

I was blessed in two respects: (1) That my mother and father decided to leave their home and move into my house during this time to attend to my needs, as I lived alone, and (2) That I wasn't paralyzed. At the time, I was told that 90% of C2 fractures either resulted in death or paralysis.

After realizing how lucky I was, I have to say I was never worried by what the future held for me. The circumstances seemed very matter of fact to me, much like they would to an athlete who suffers a broken leg and knows he must go through the process of first allowing it to heal and then rehabbing it.

To me, it was a matter of consciously "being in the moment." Alright, what do we do now? What is the process for working through *this* situation?

It was like the sight of a football player being carted off the field on a stretcher, and as he's being pushed into the tunnel, he raises a hand with his thumb thrust into the air as if to say, "I've got this. It's going to be okay."

The playbook on how to mentally approach sports worked for me during that personal crisis and my subsequent recuperation. I was fortunate to completely recover without any permanent effects of the accident. And after five months of healing, recovery, and rehab, I returned to the job, and life, I loved.

Perhaps the sports mindset can work for you, too?

Just put in the work, treat others with respect, follow the right processes, concentrate on drills that will build your skills and your self-confidence, play by the rules, respect the established social structure, rely on the advantages you have, be committed and disciplined, and become a star in your role.

And to quote my sportswriter friend Loren Ledin, "Remember, the single most important lesson in sports is you can't always win. If you can get over the fear of losing, you can be a true winner. Because in dealing with failure, you learn how to succeed."

We witness those lessons—and observe those established practices—every day in the world of sports. And they can assist us, as well, in the daily things we do.

One of America's superstars of personal development was a man named Jim Rohn. Rohn began his professional career as a human resources manager for Sears department stores and spent more than forty years as an author, entrepreneur, astute mentor of personal development, and a much sought-after motivational speaker who traveled the world to produce the seminar series called "Adventures in Achievement."

Rohn would often wrap up his seminars with this fantastic sports-focused declaration:

"At the end of this life, let it show your runs, your hits, your errors. The times when you hit a home run. The times you struck out. But don't let it show you haven't played. How would you explain that?"

In closing, sports can offer us many things—exercise, entertainment, a career, a place to invest our rooting interests, and sometimes a relief from life's daily challenges.

Most importantly, sports can offer us examples of how to meet those challenges. I hope this book has inspired you to create a lifetime of winning "highlight reel" moments as you abide by your own Playbook for Success.